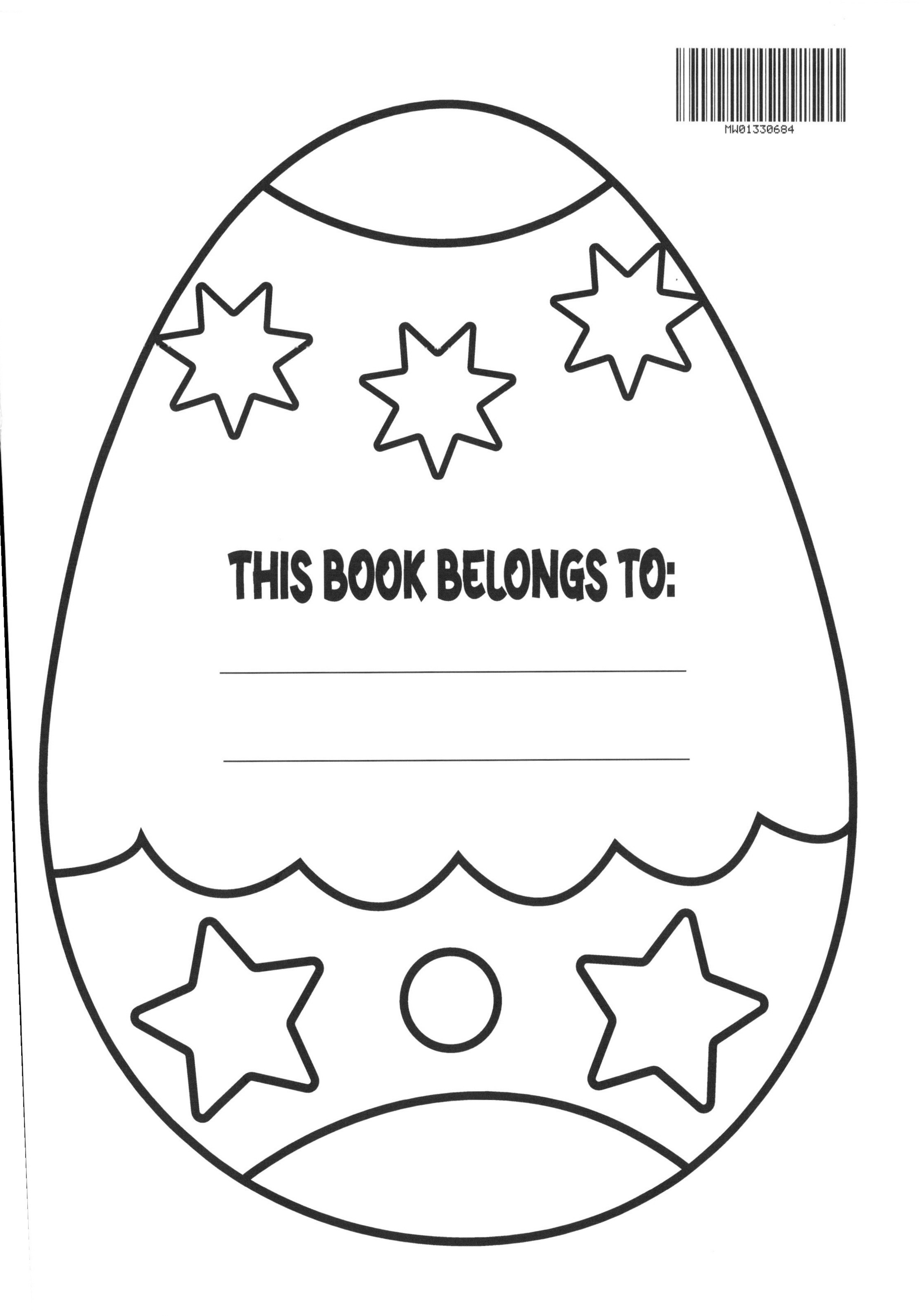
THIS BOOK BELONGS TO:

For any inquiries or questions regarding our books,
please contact us at : masumkha71@gmail.com

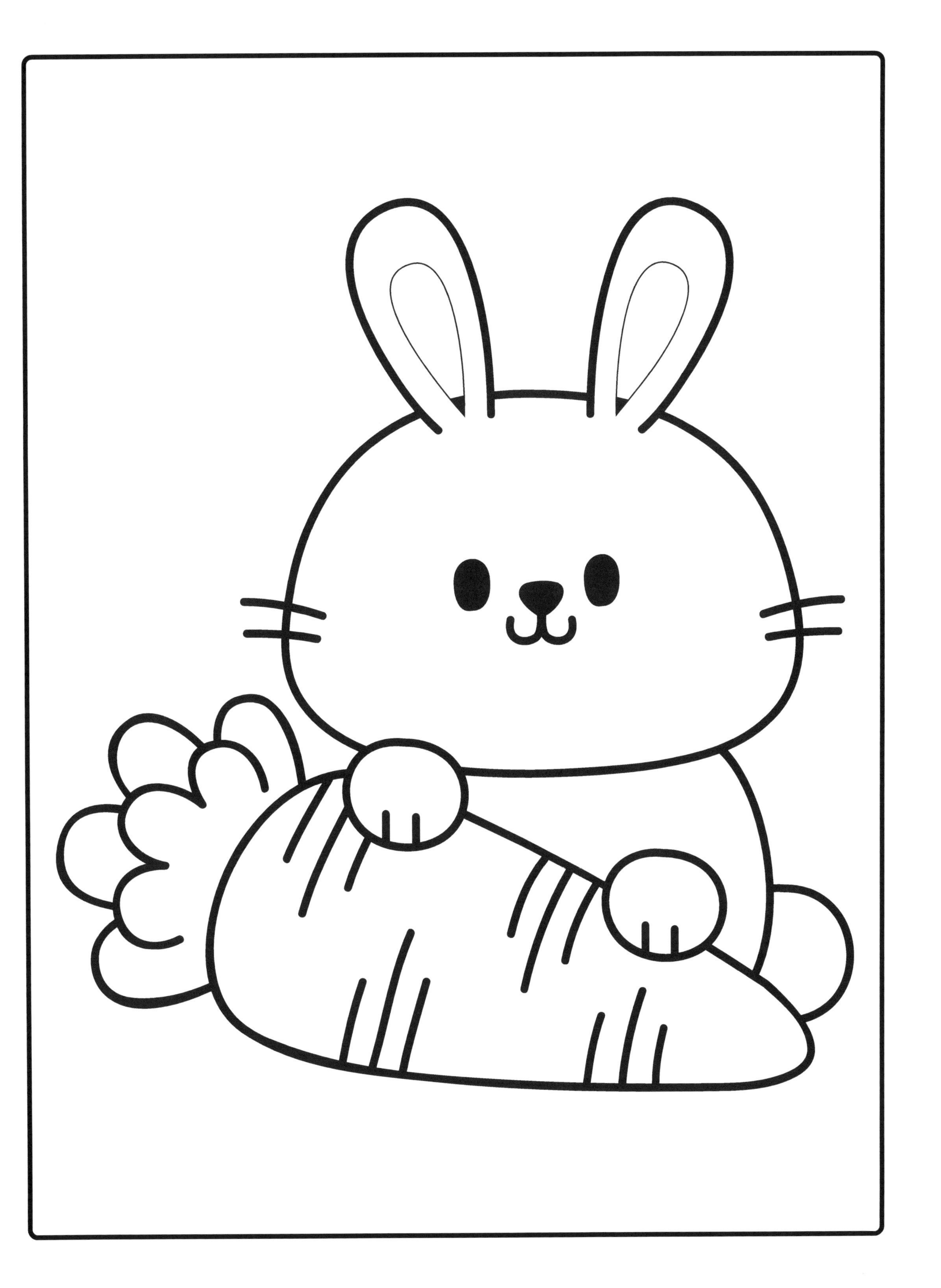

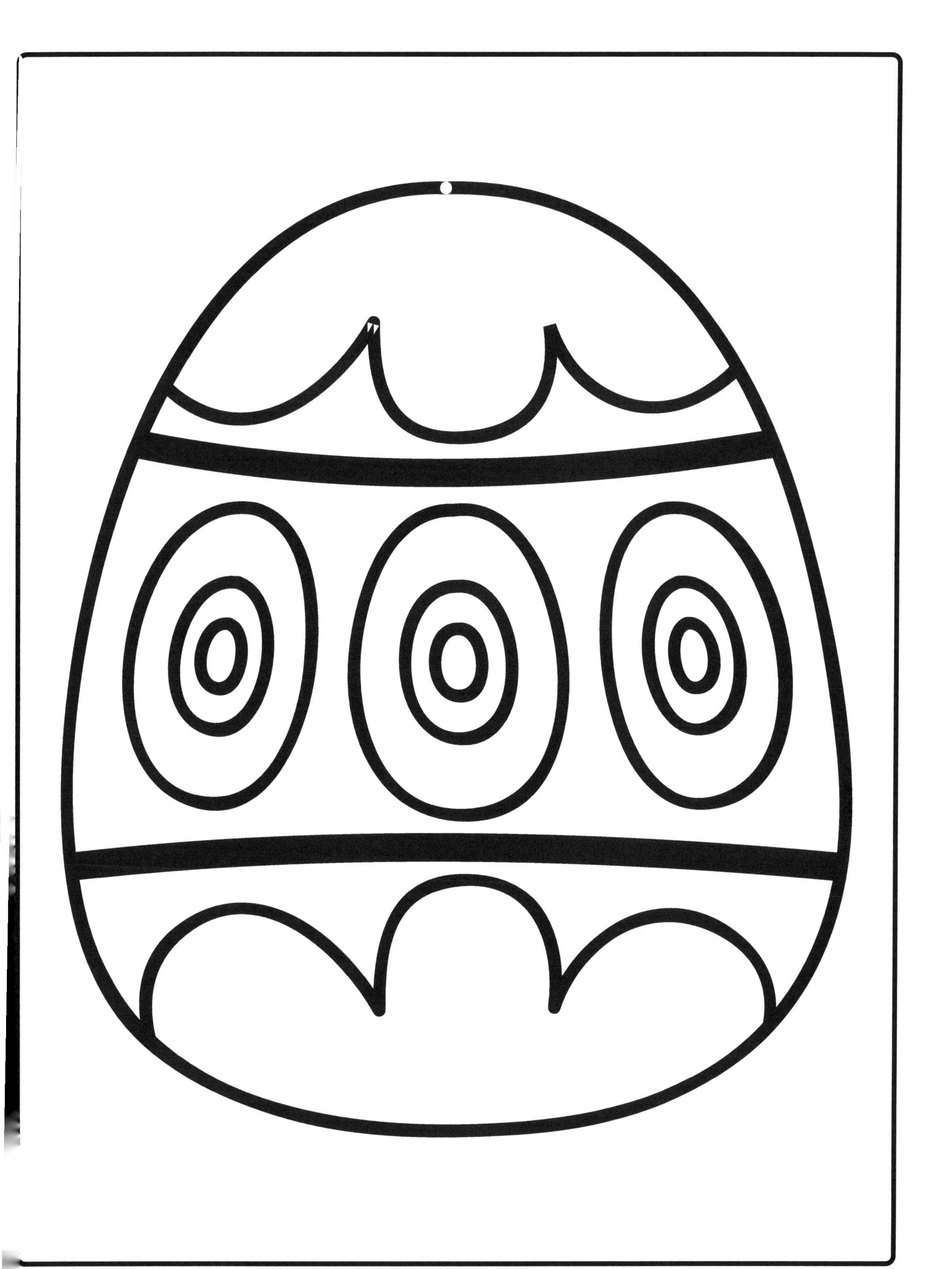

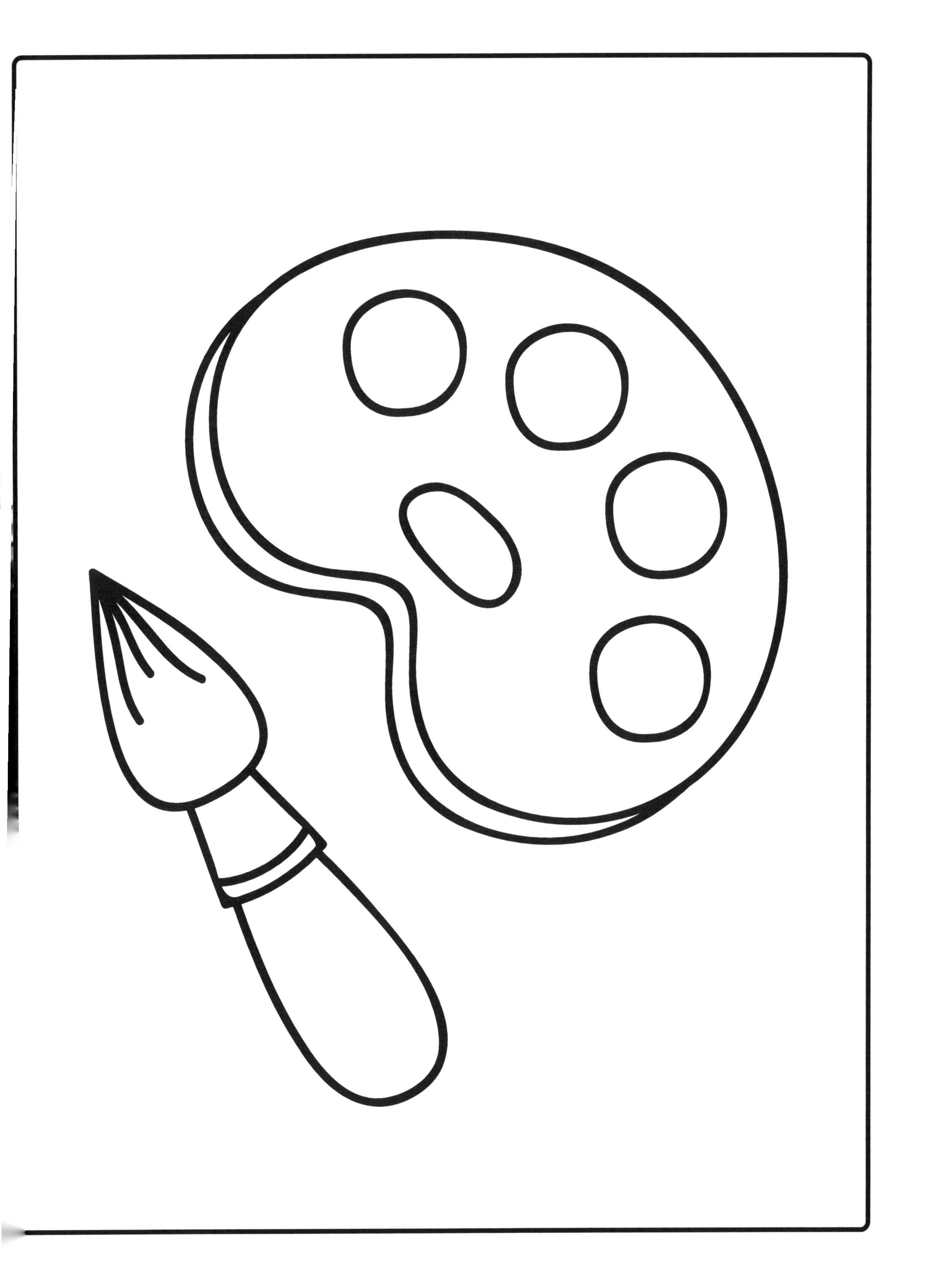

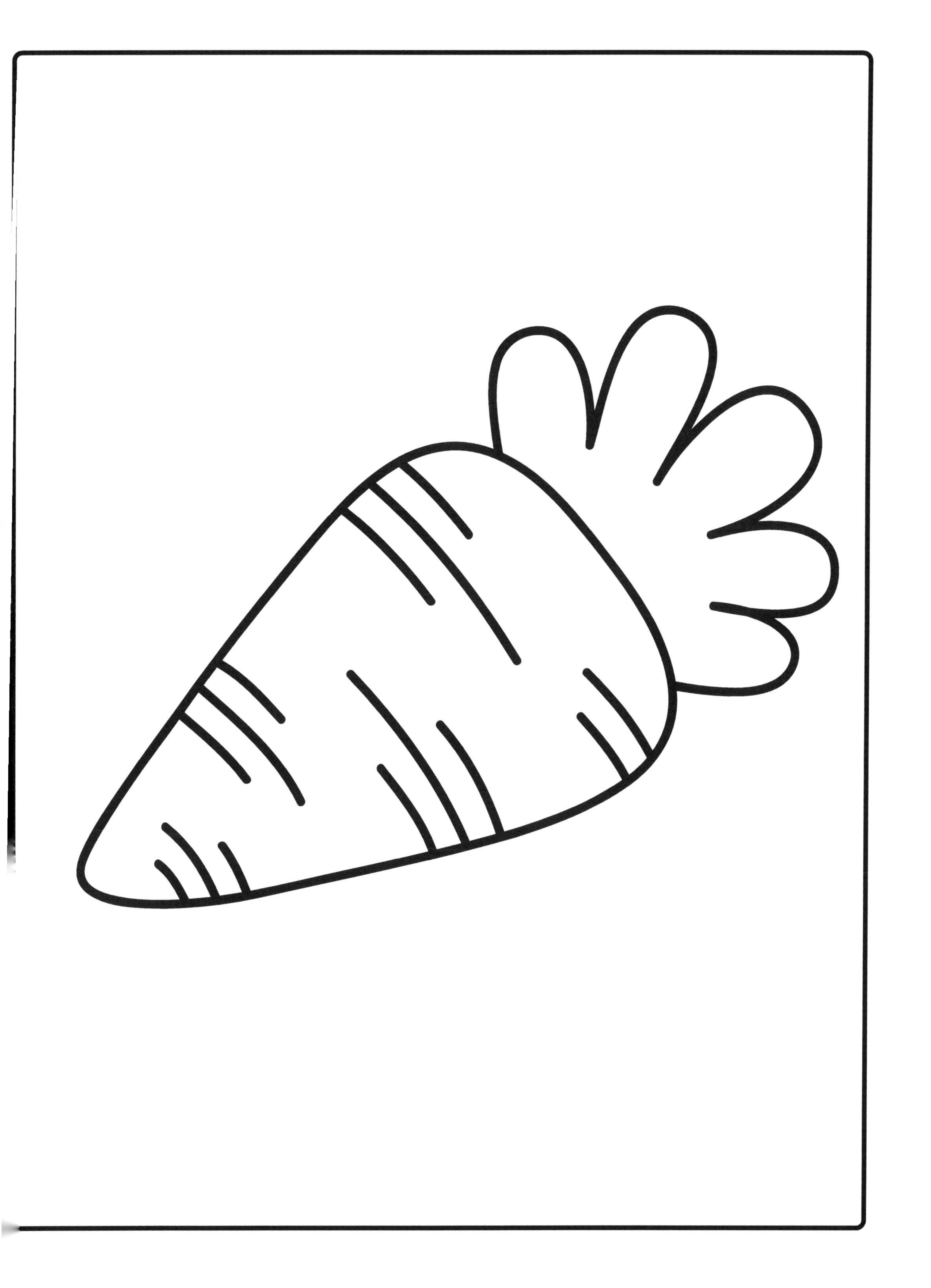

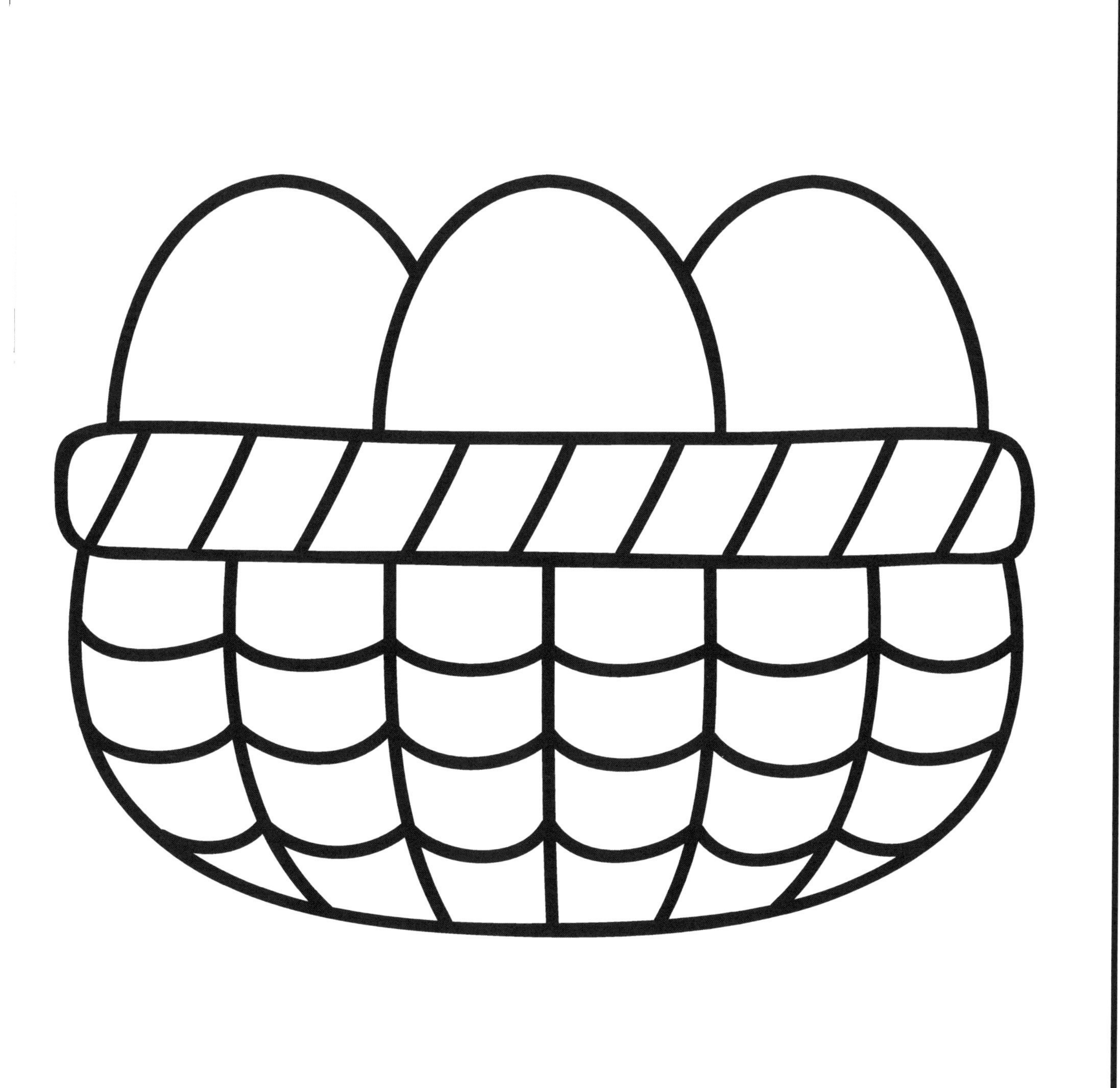

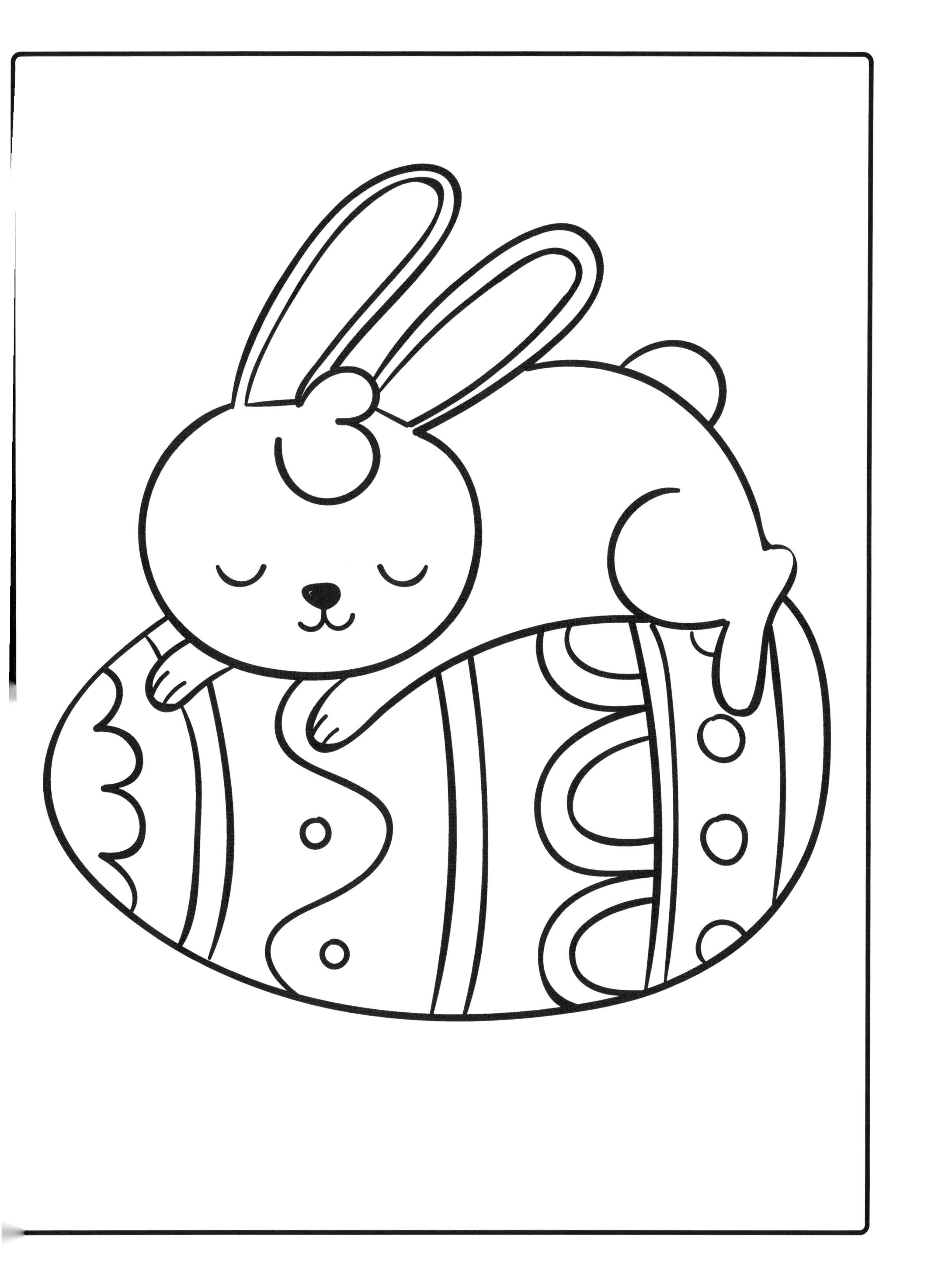

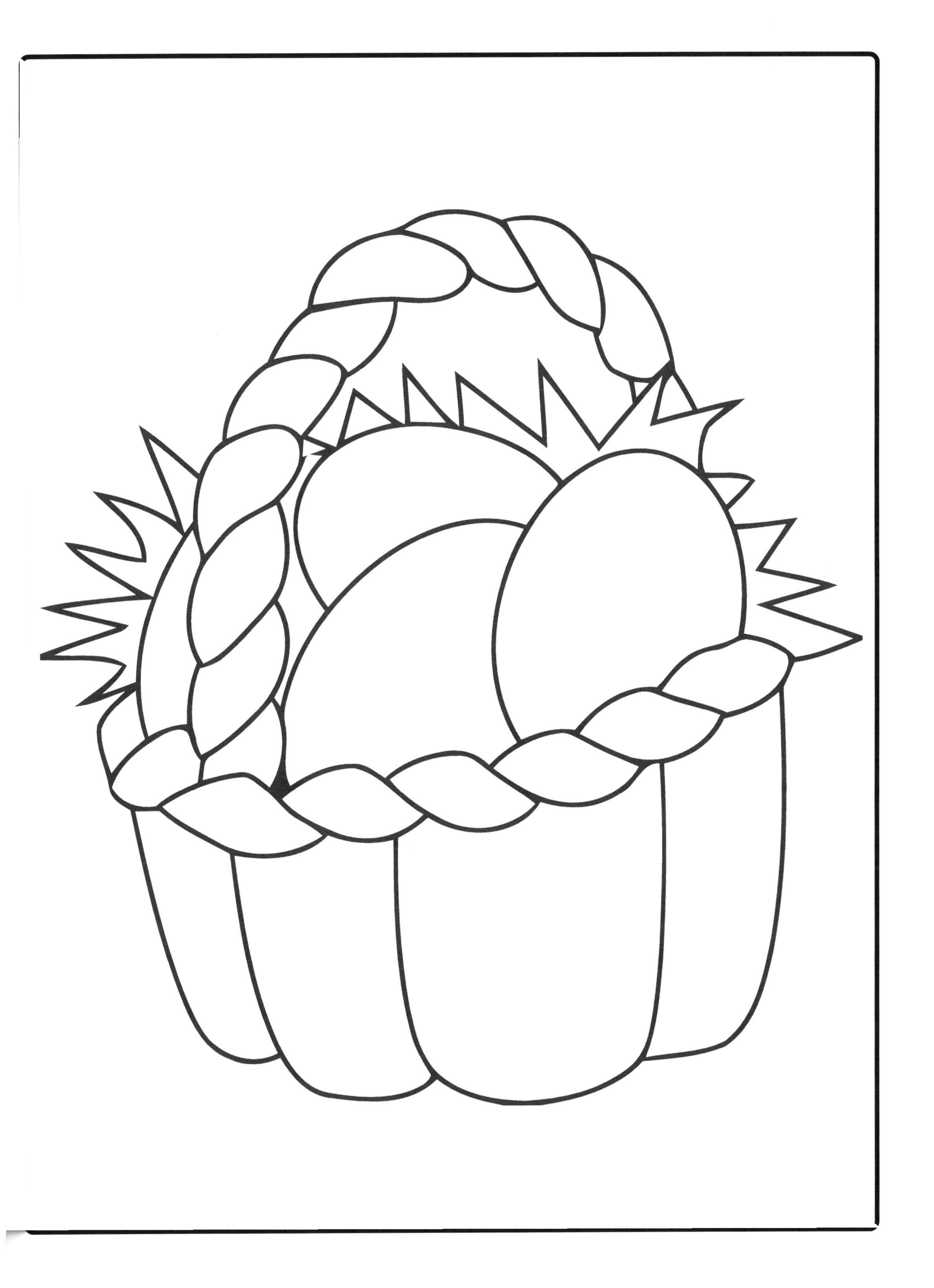

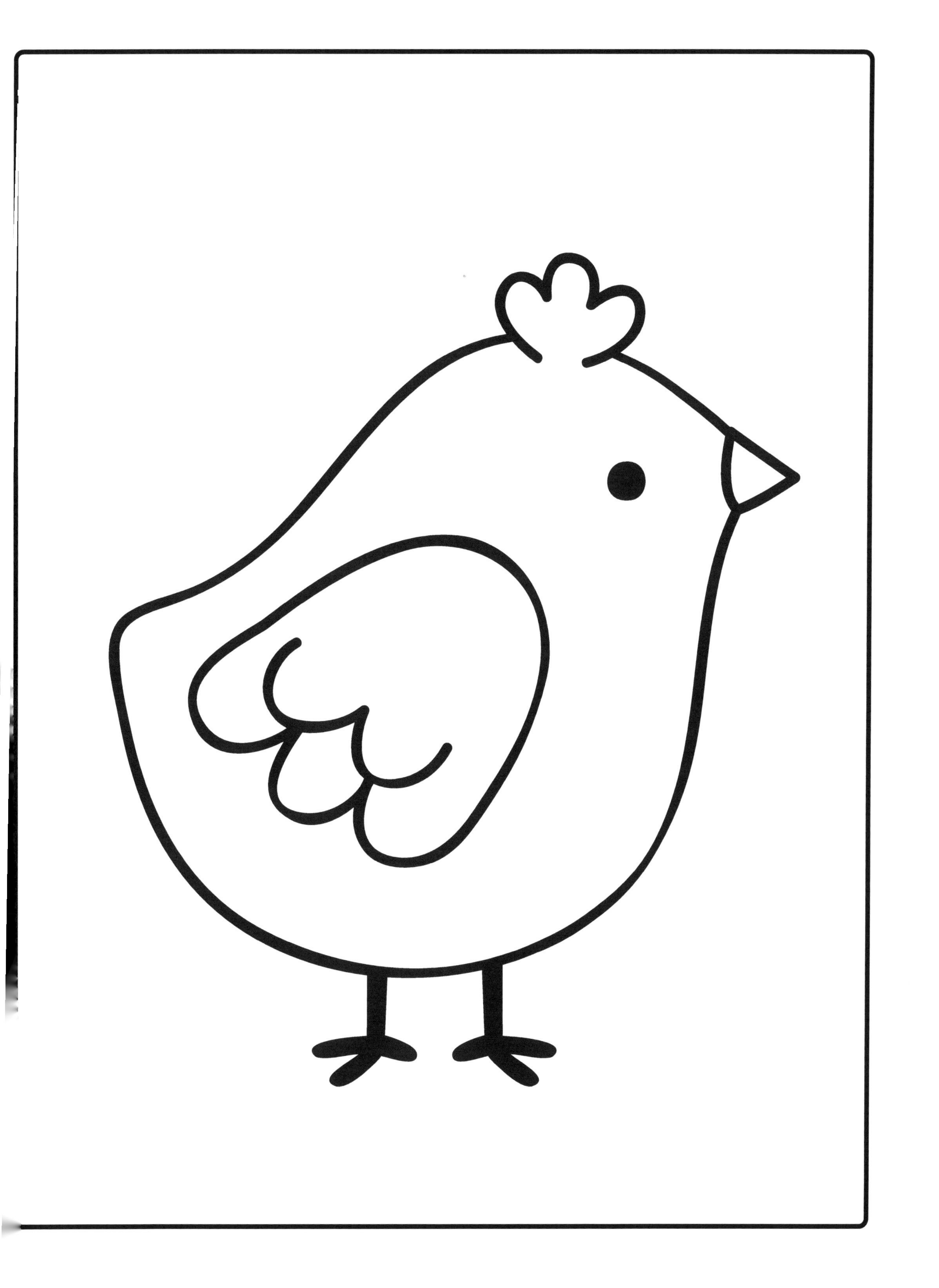

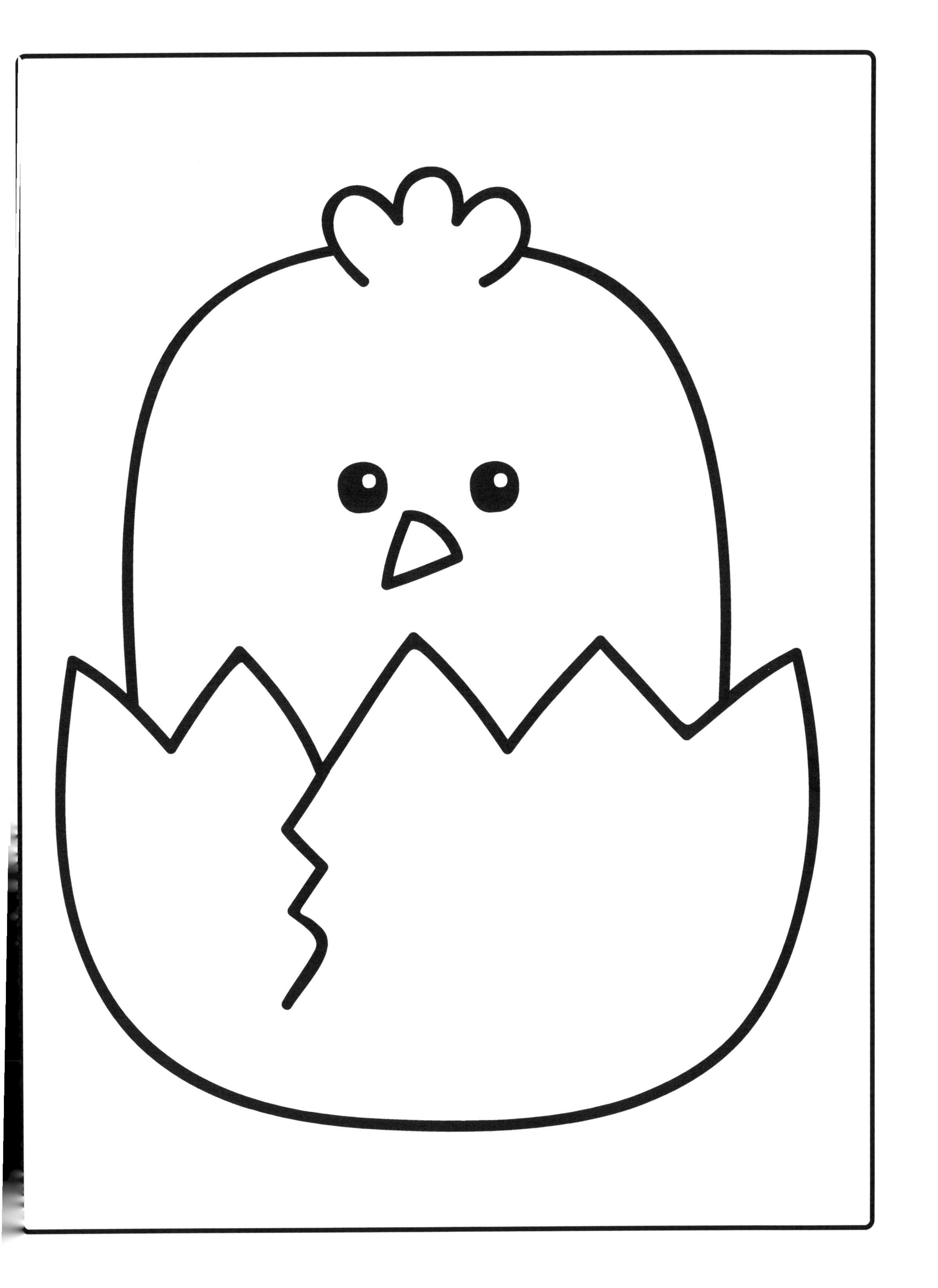

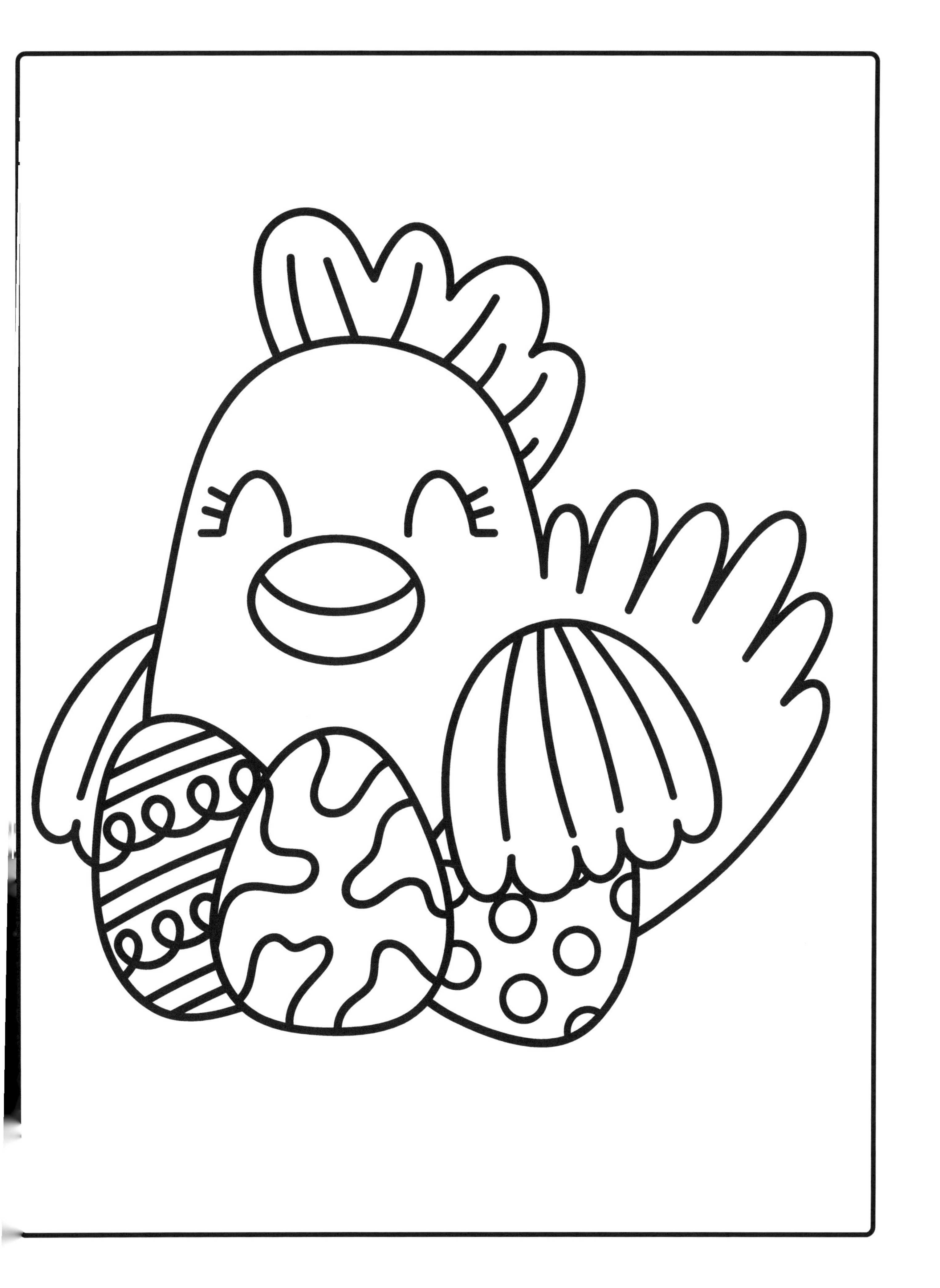

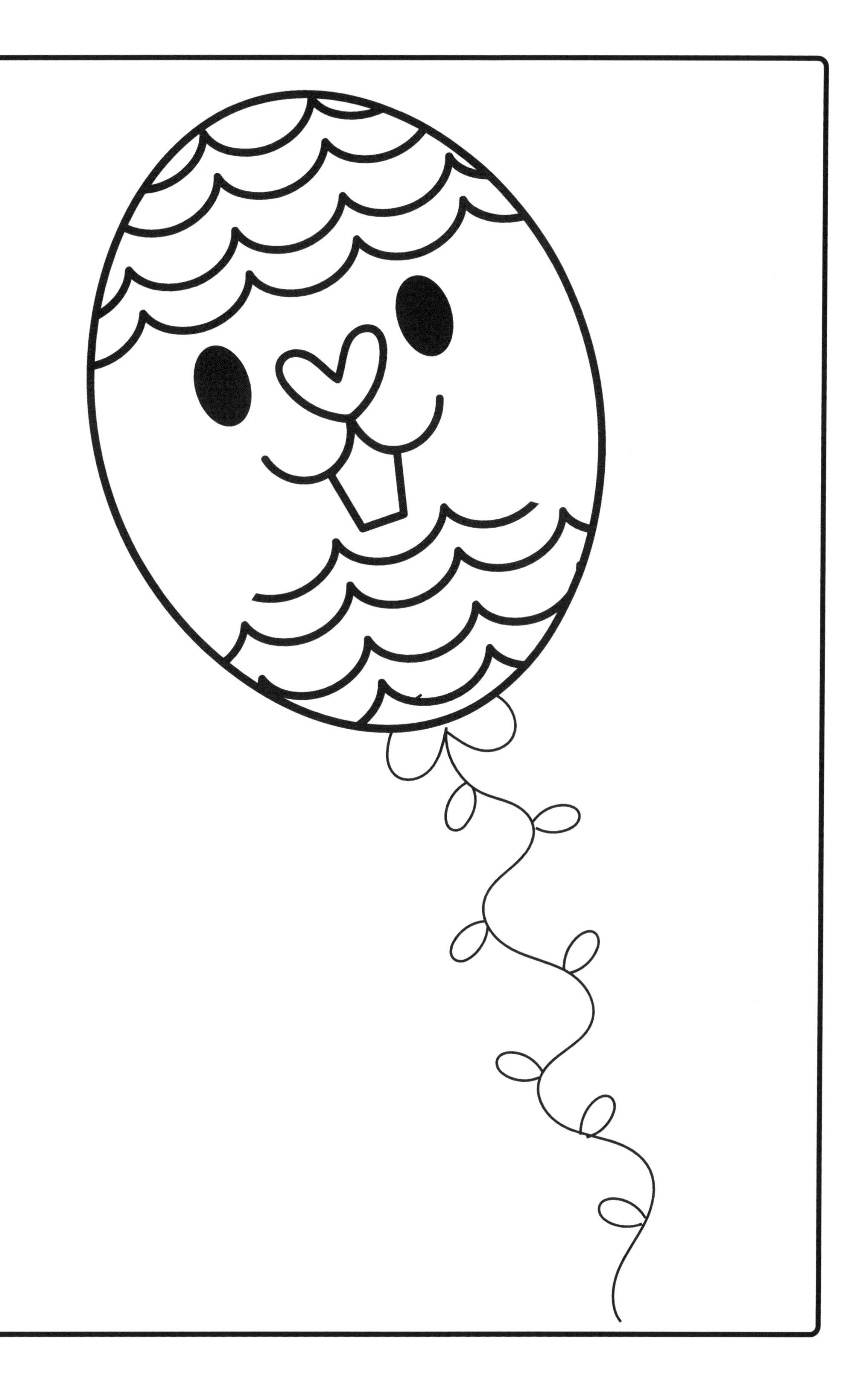

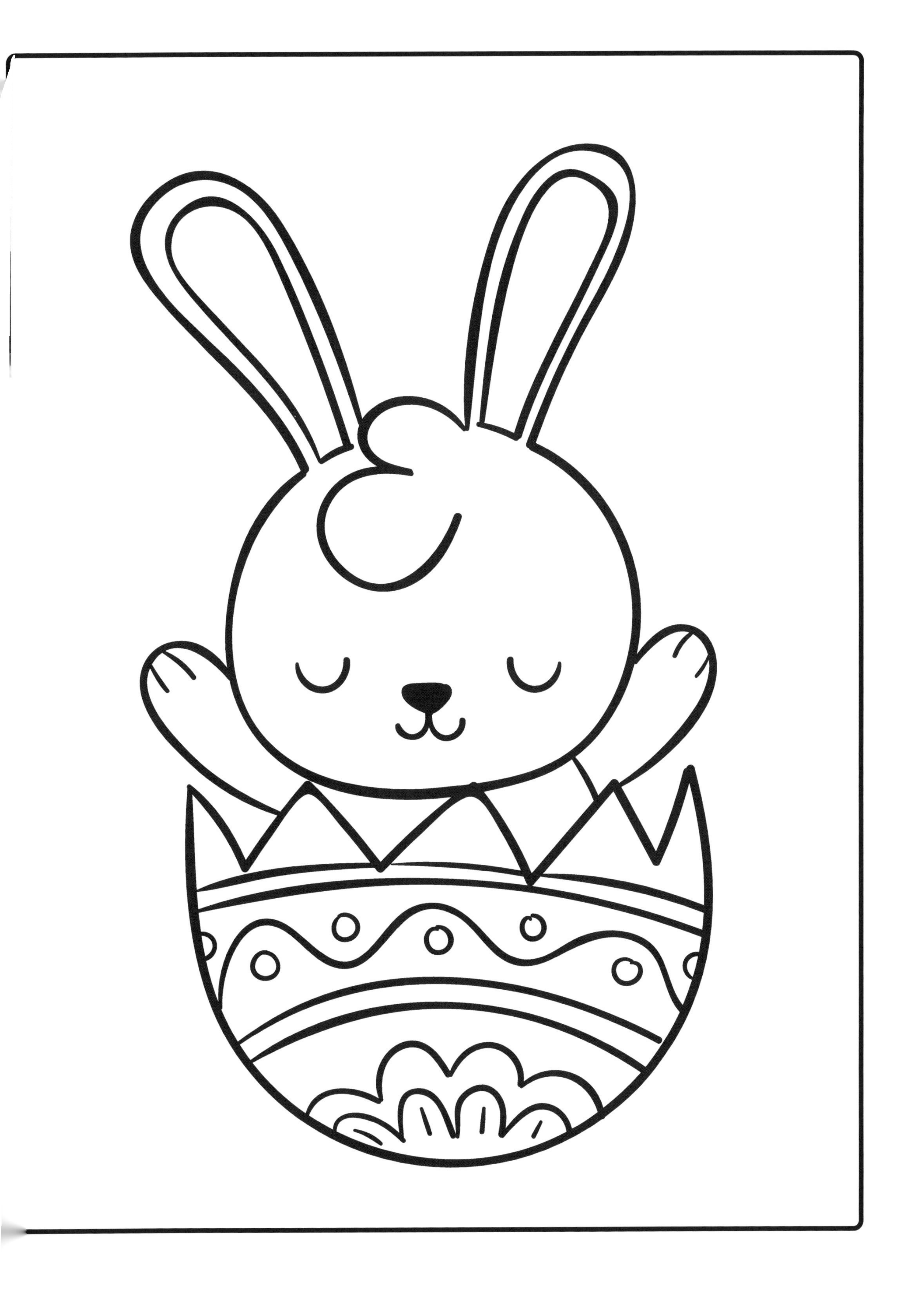

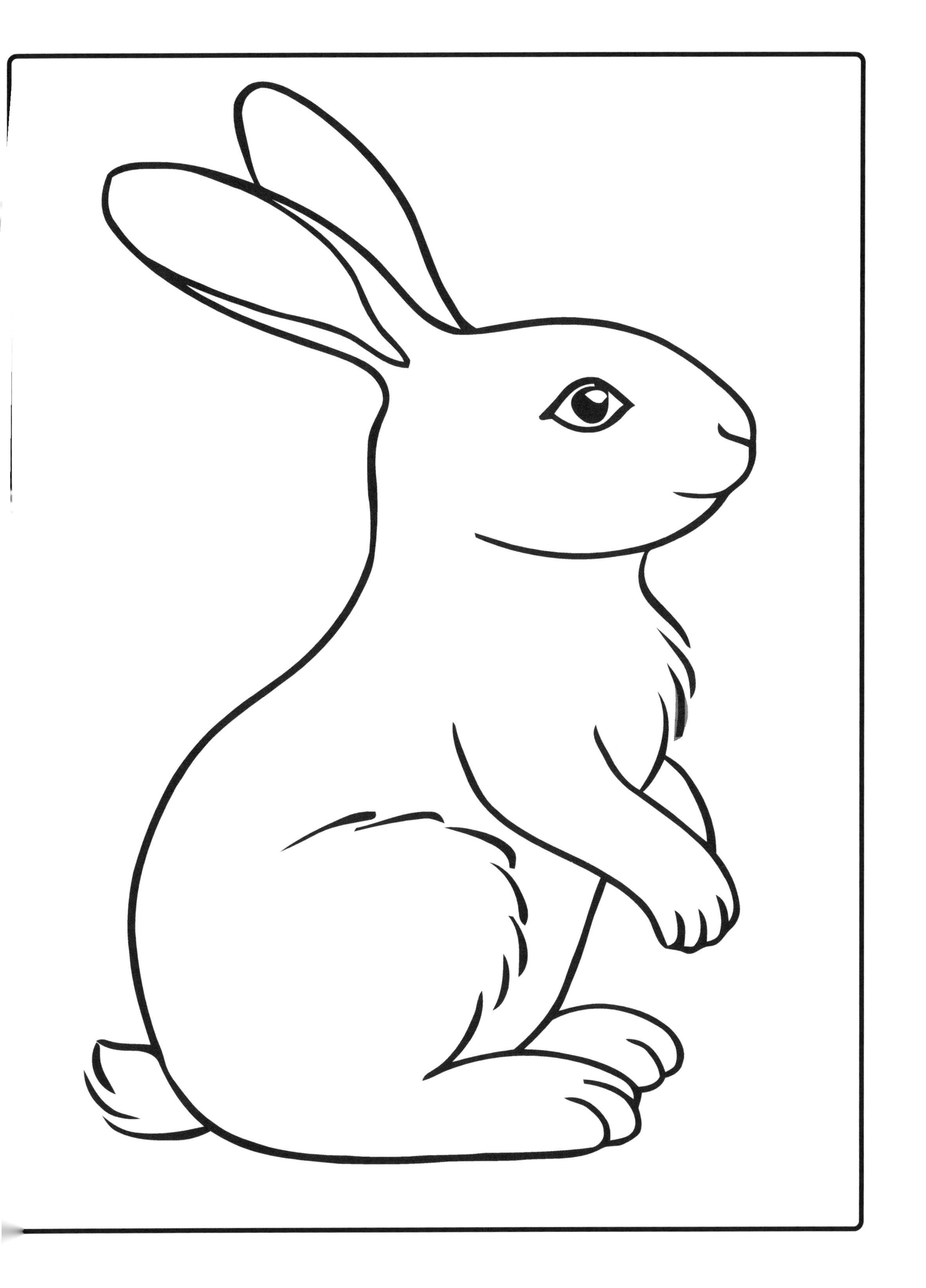

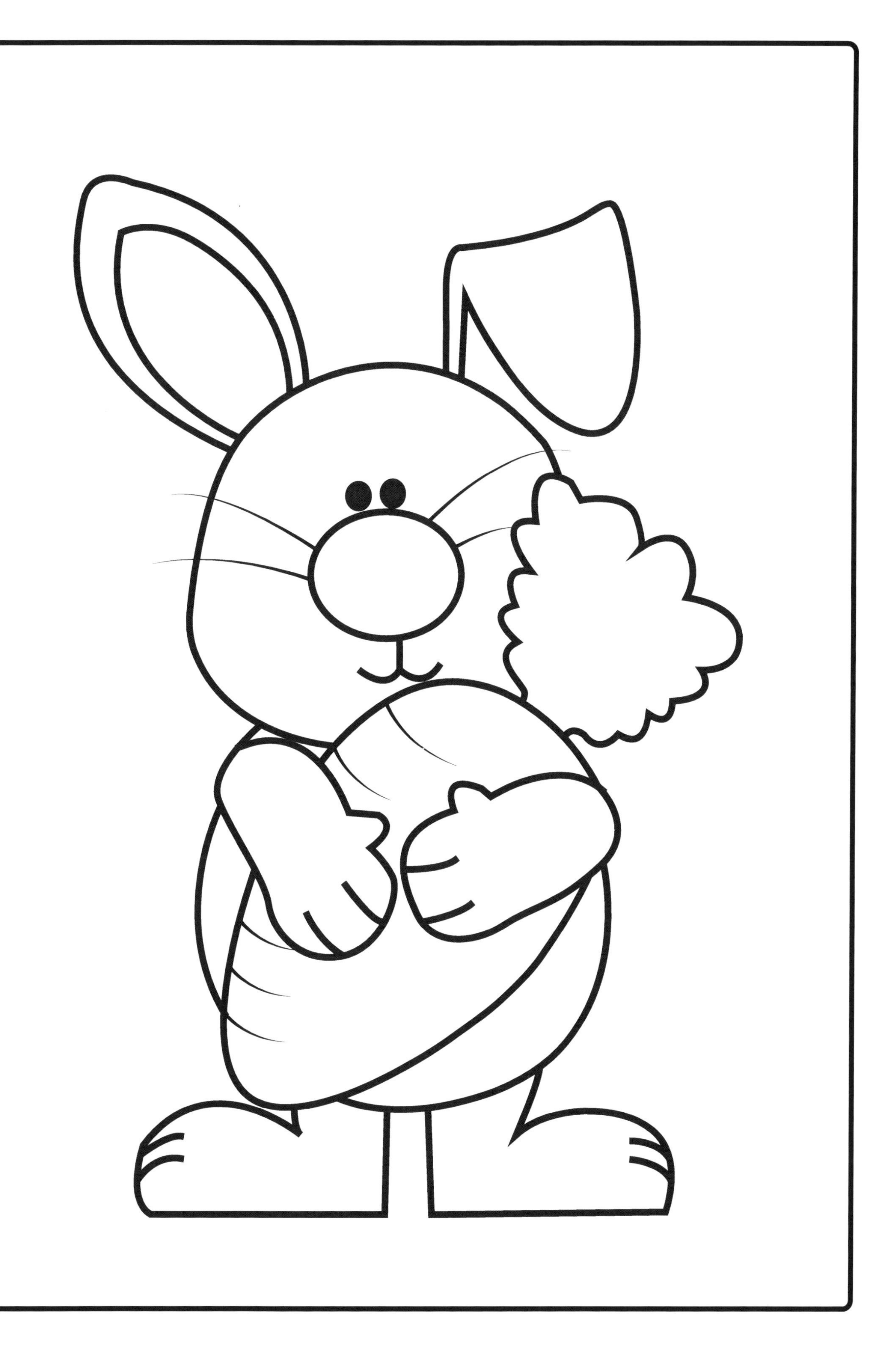

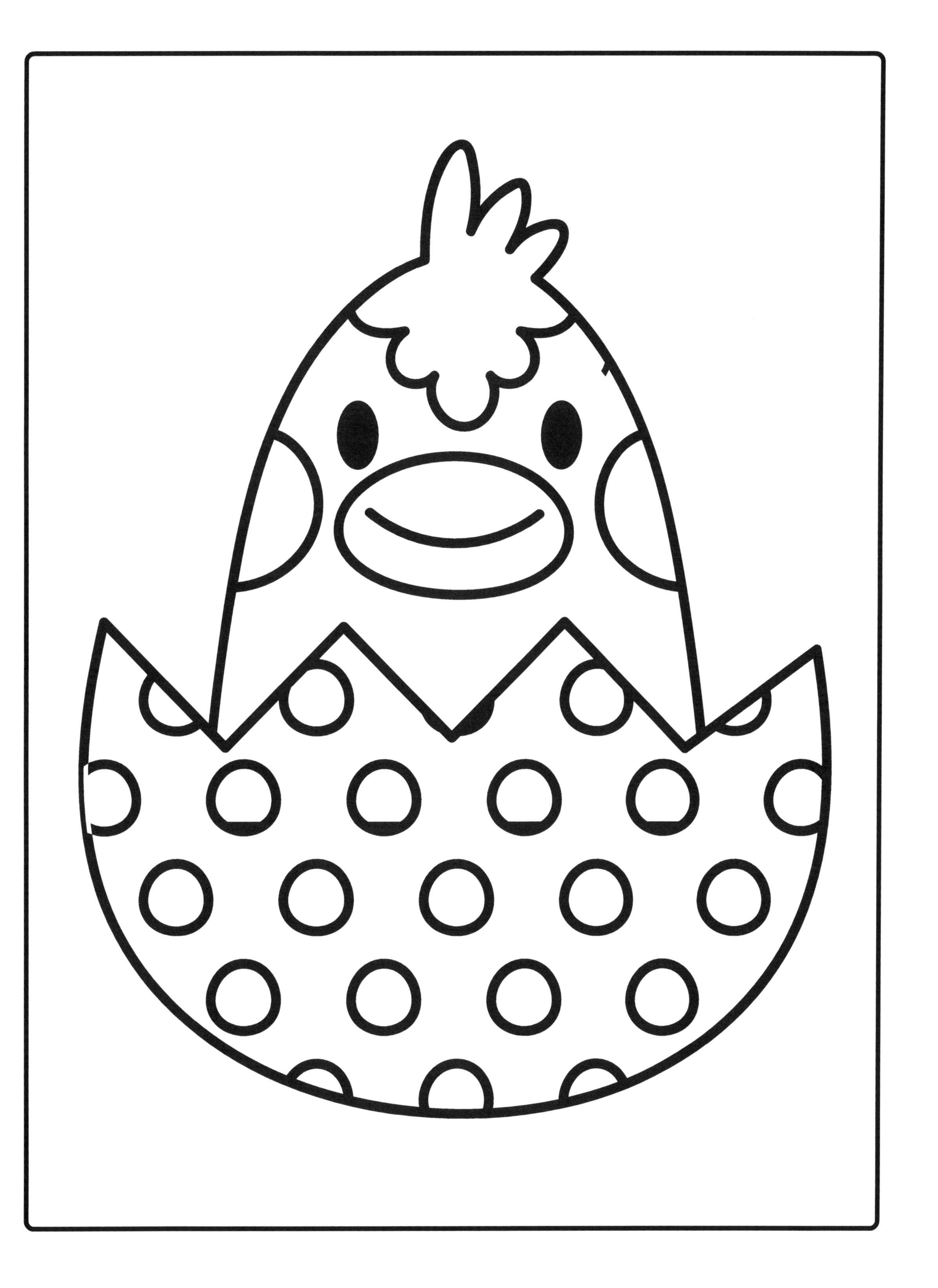

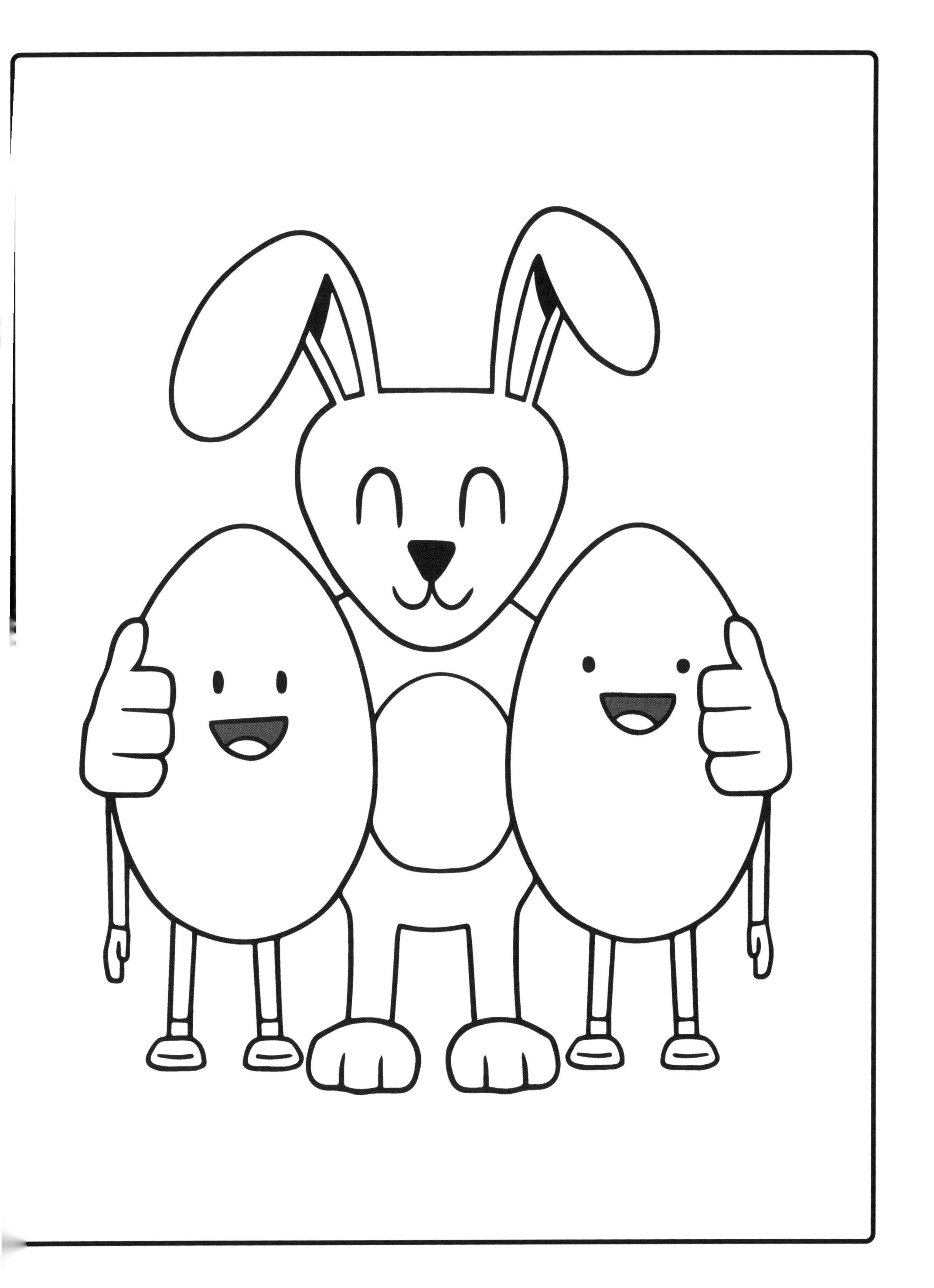

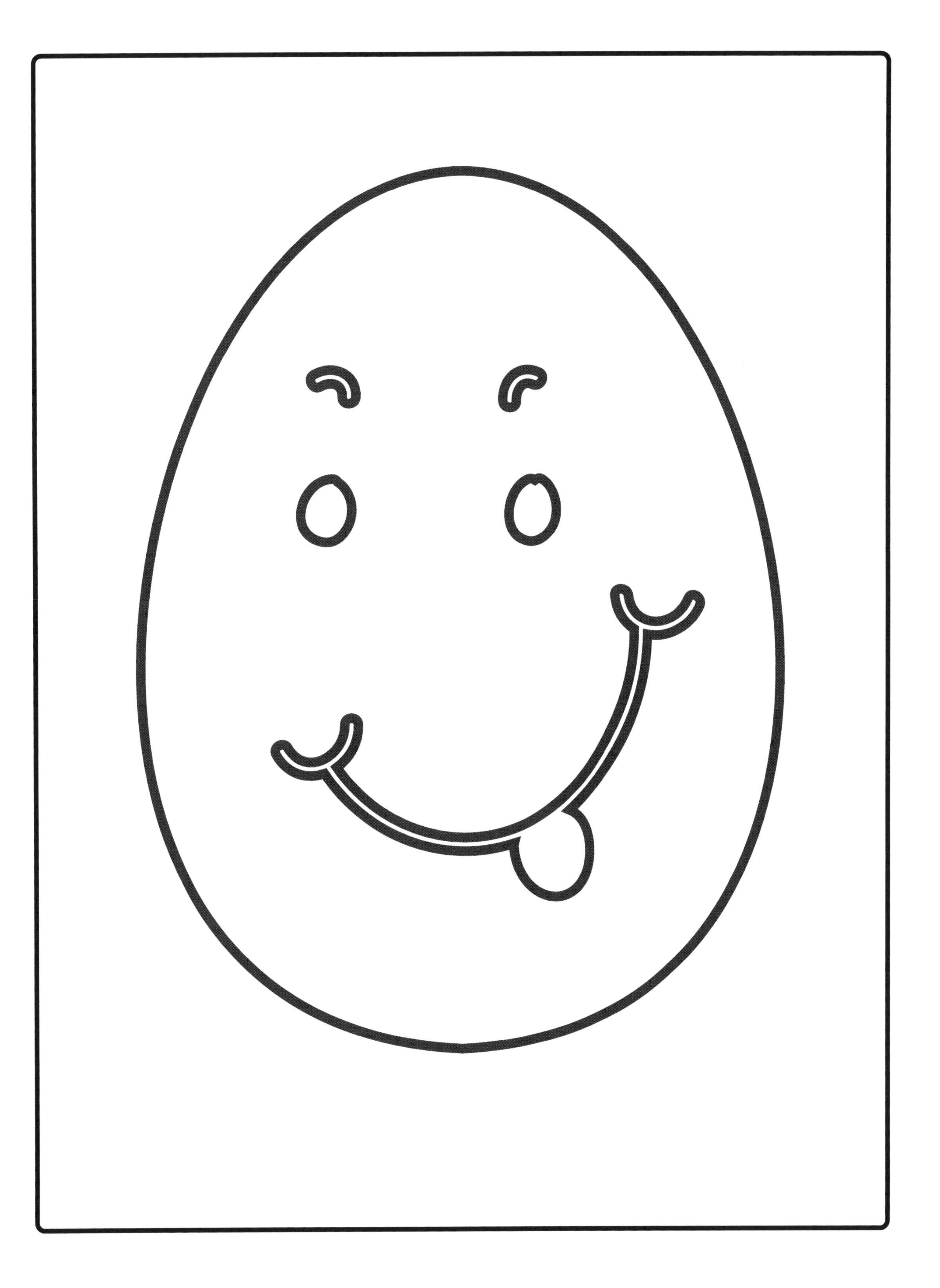

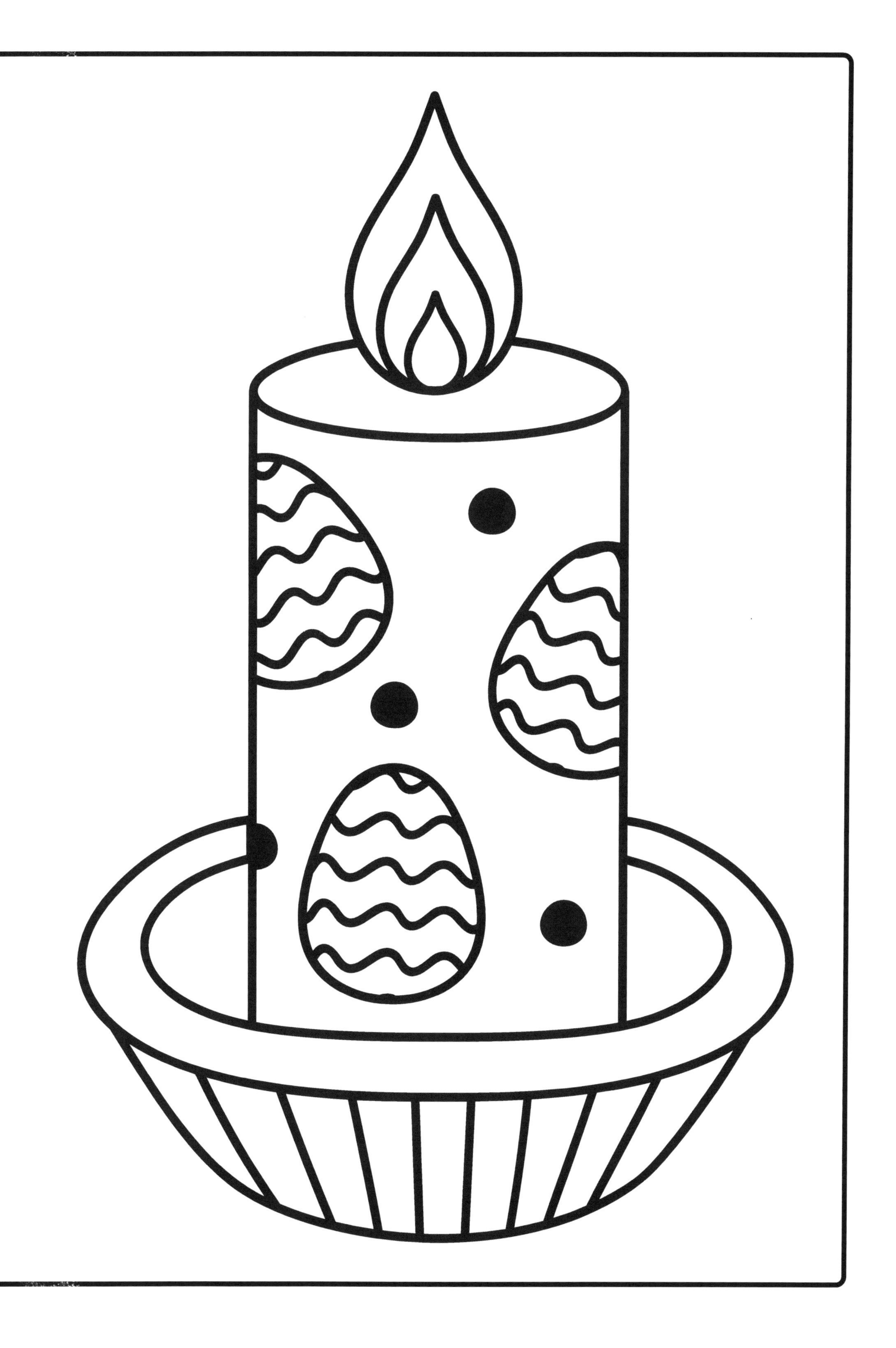

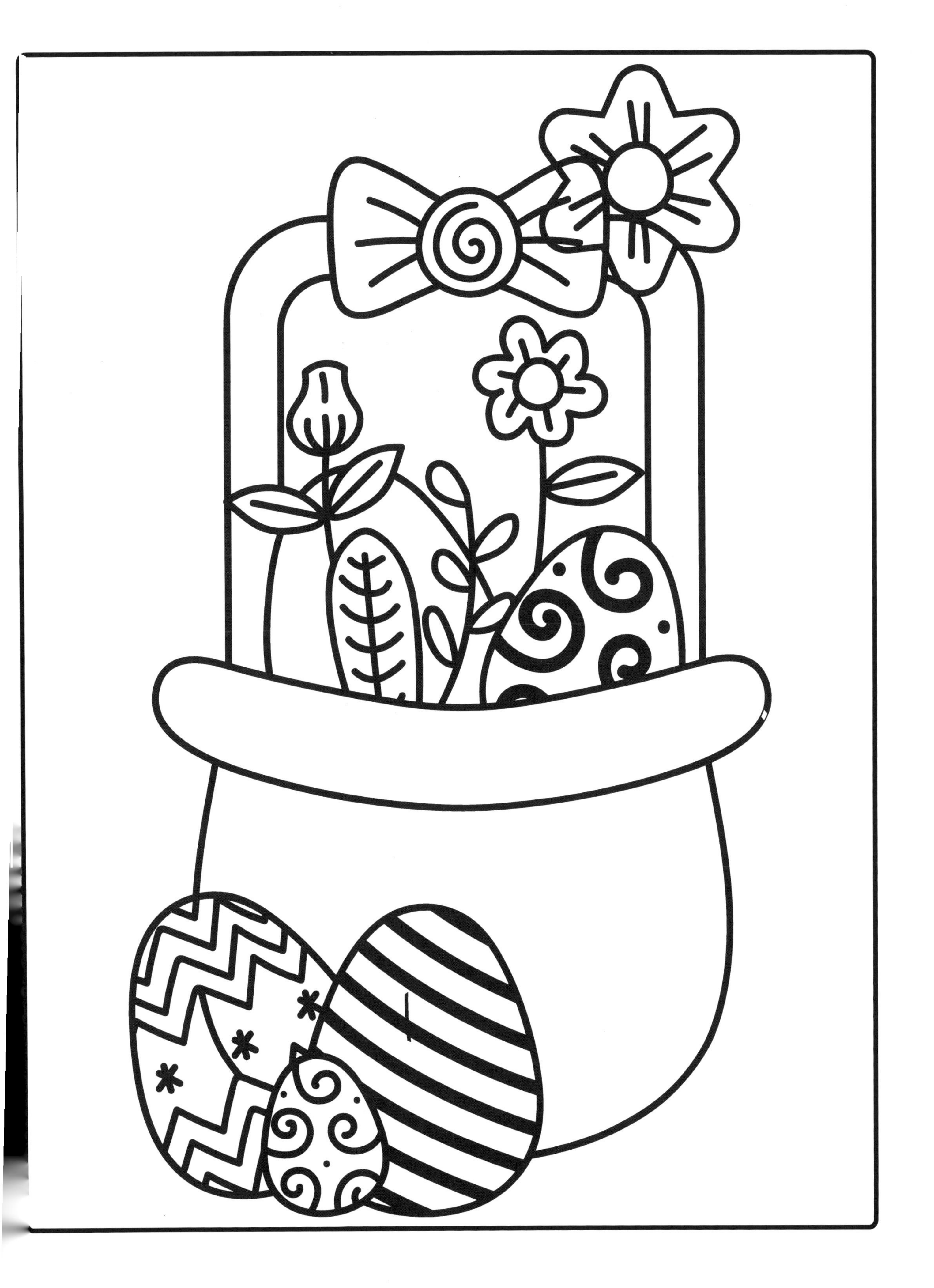

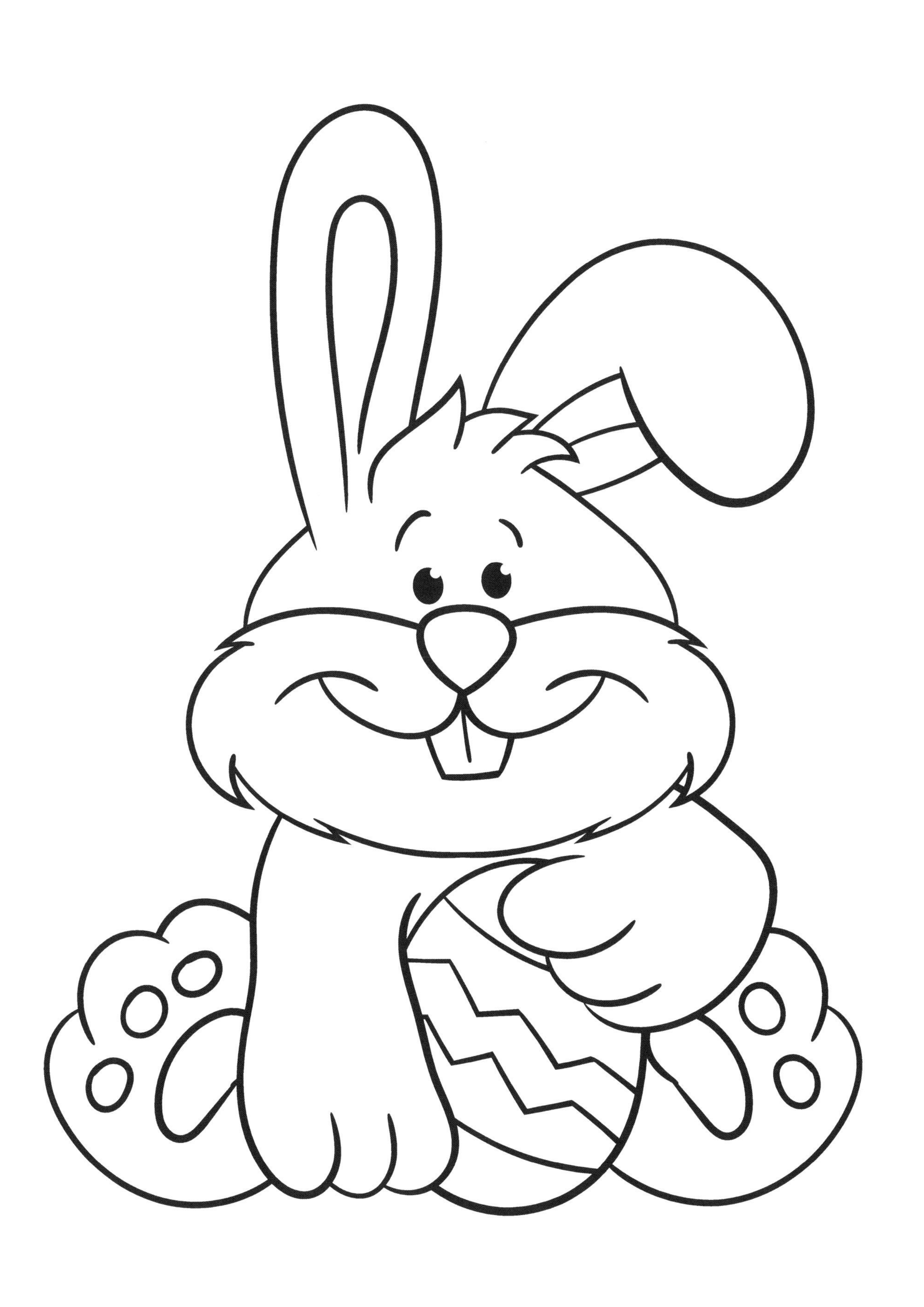

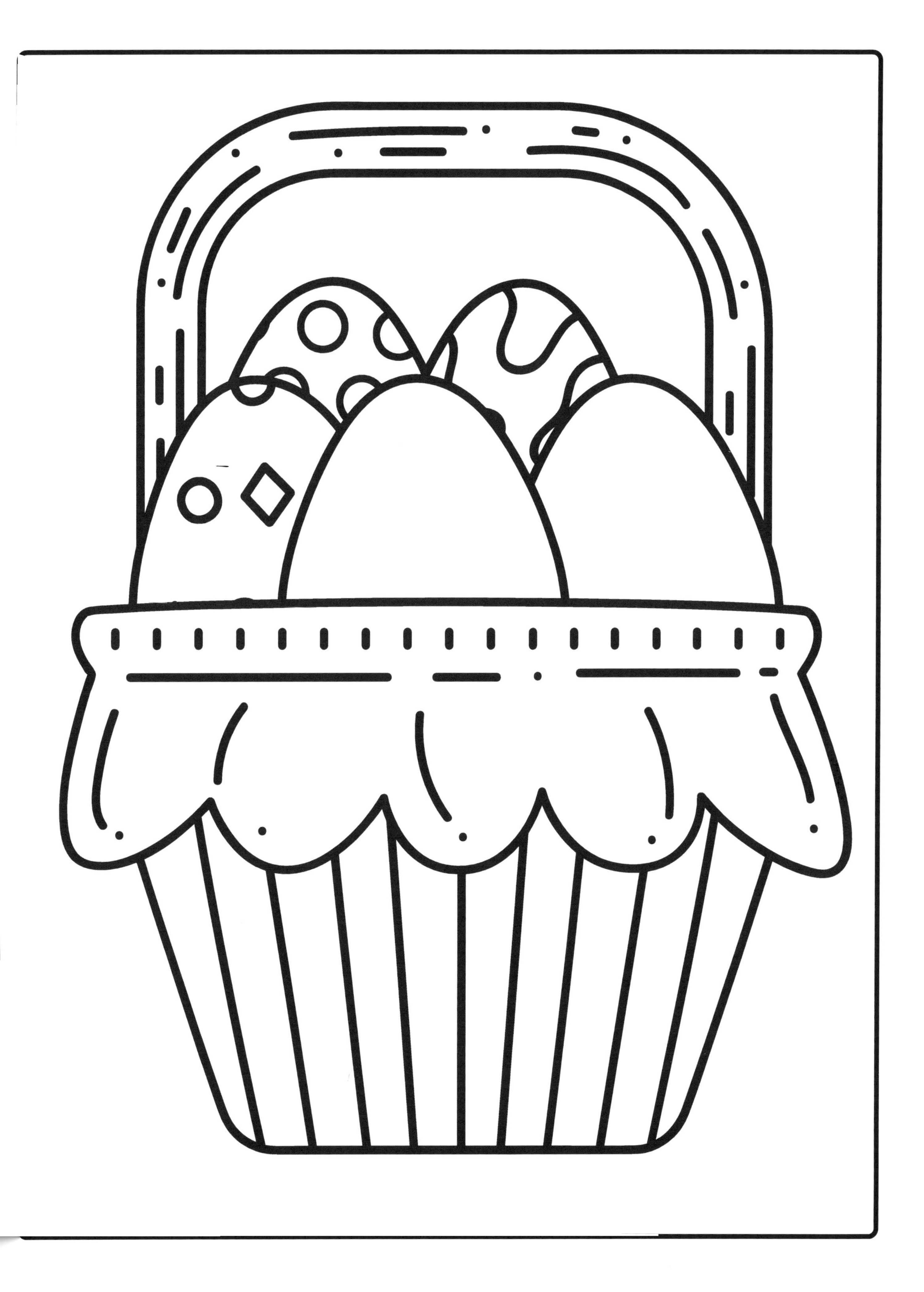

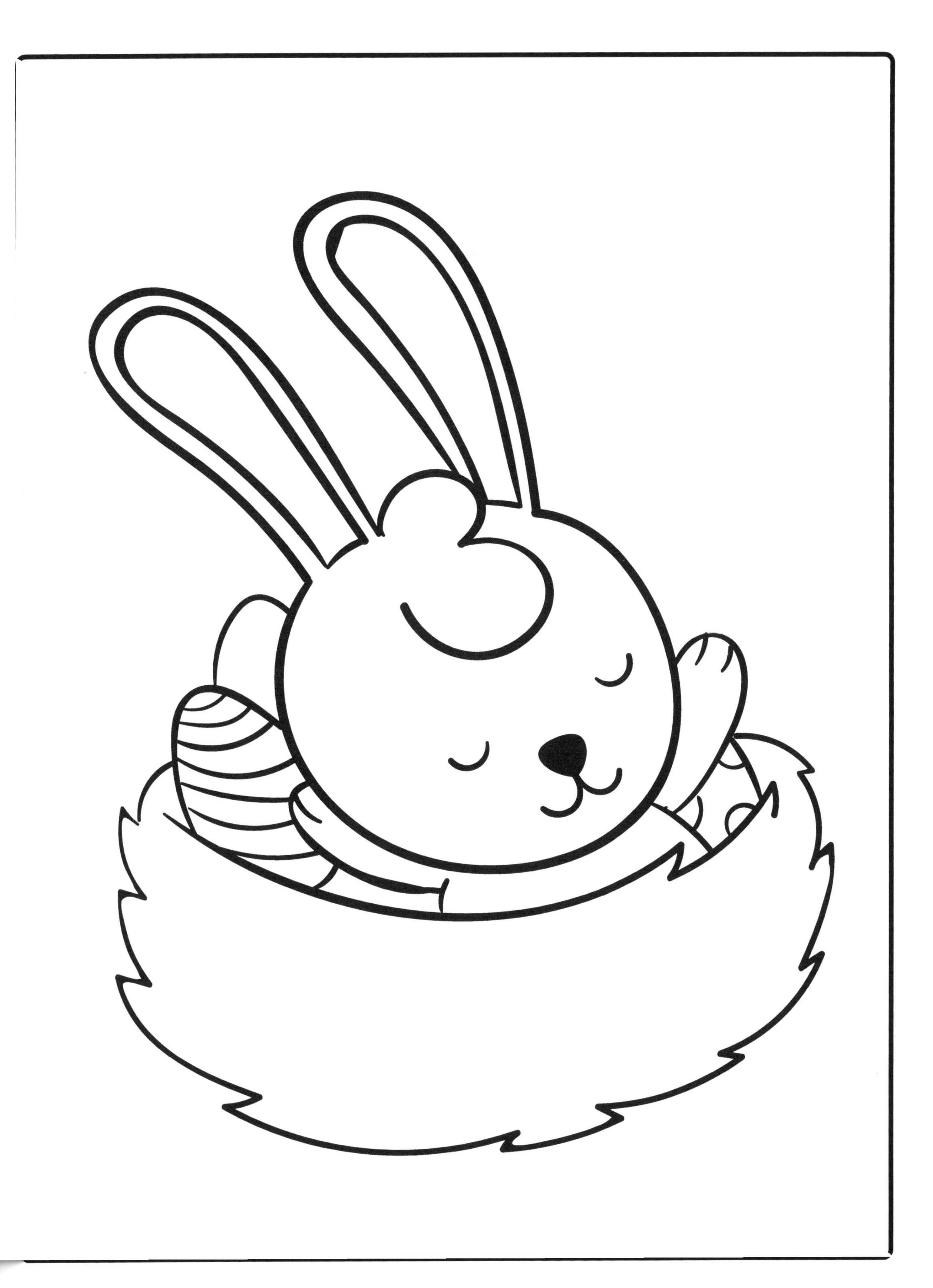

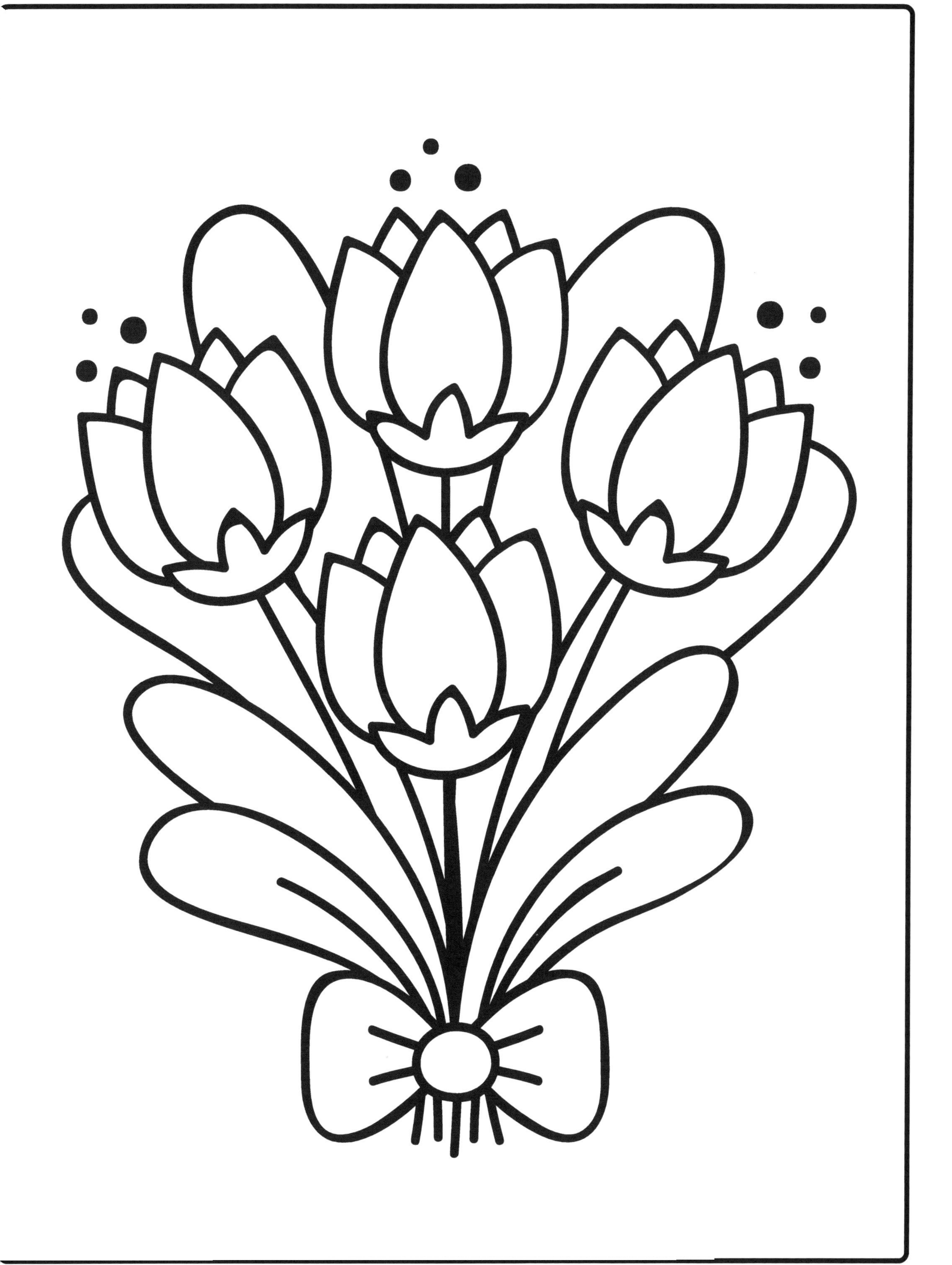

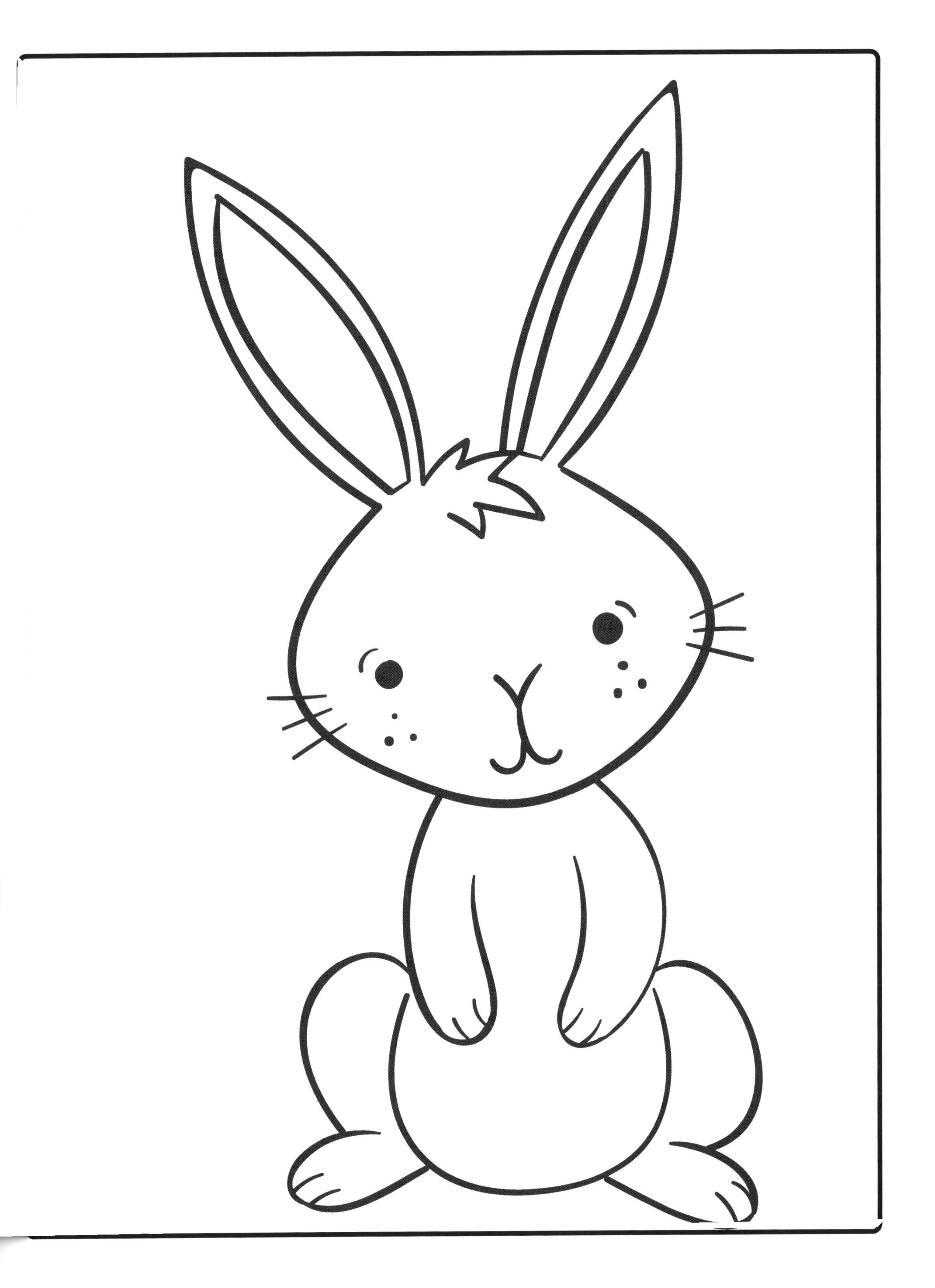

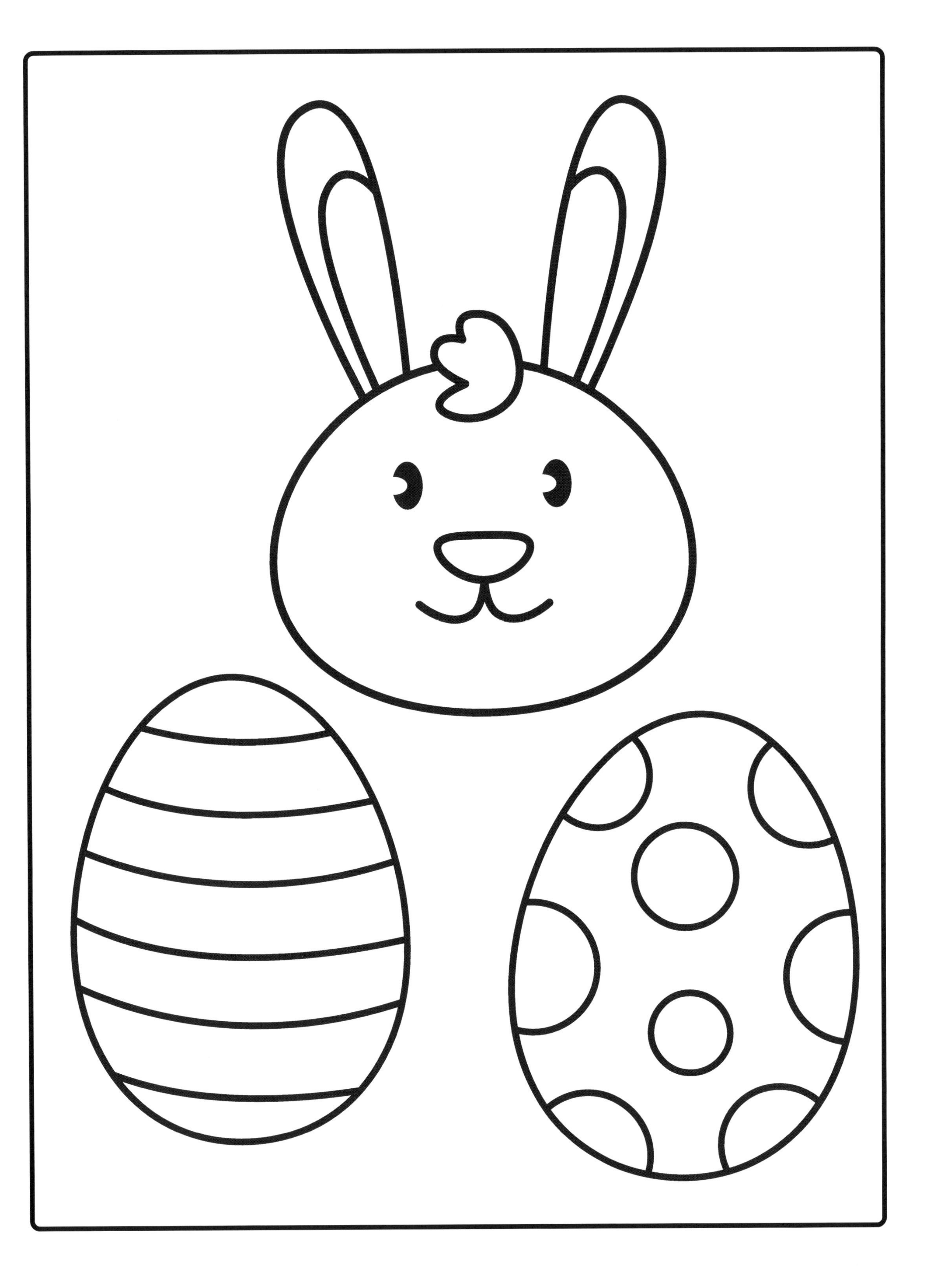

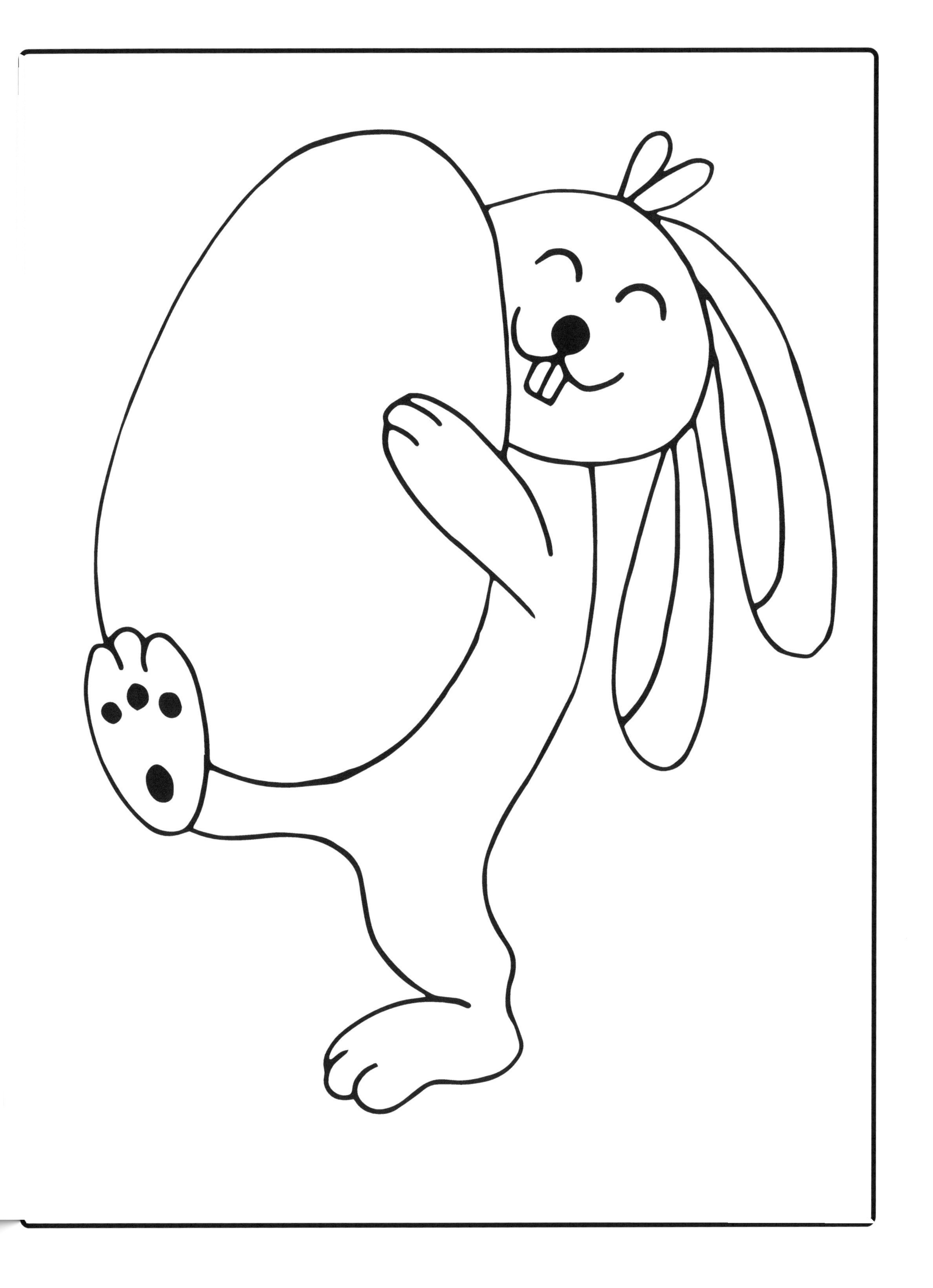

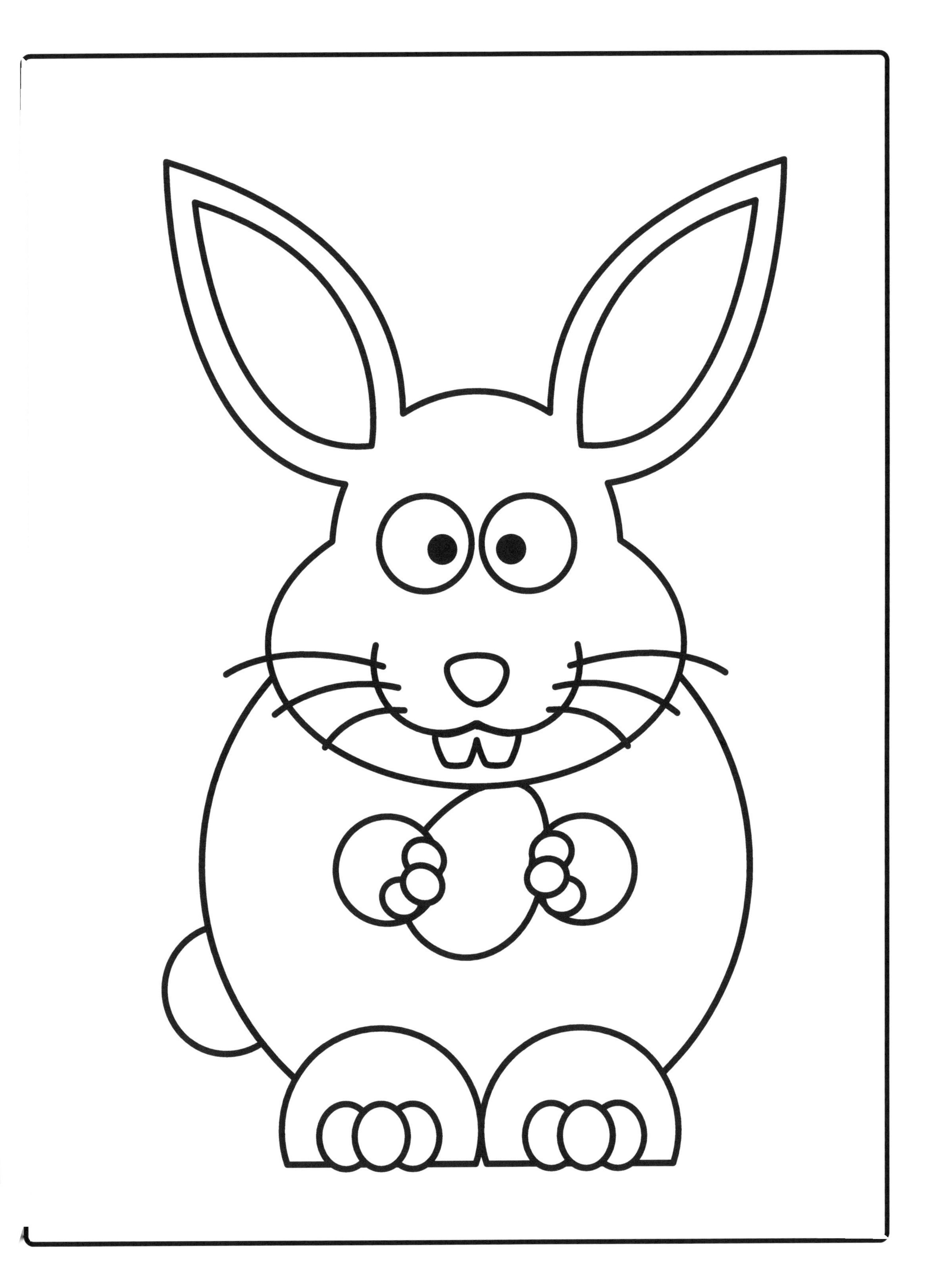

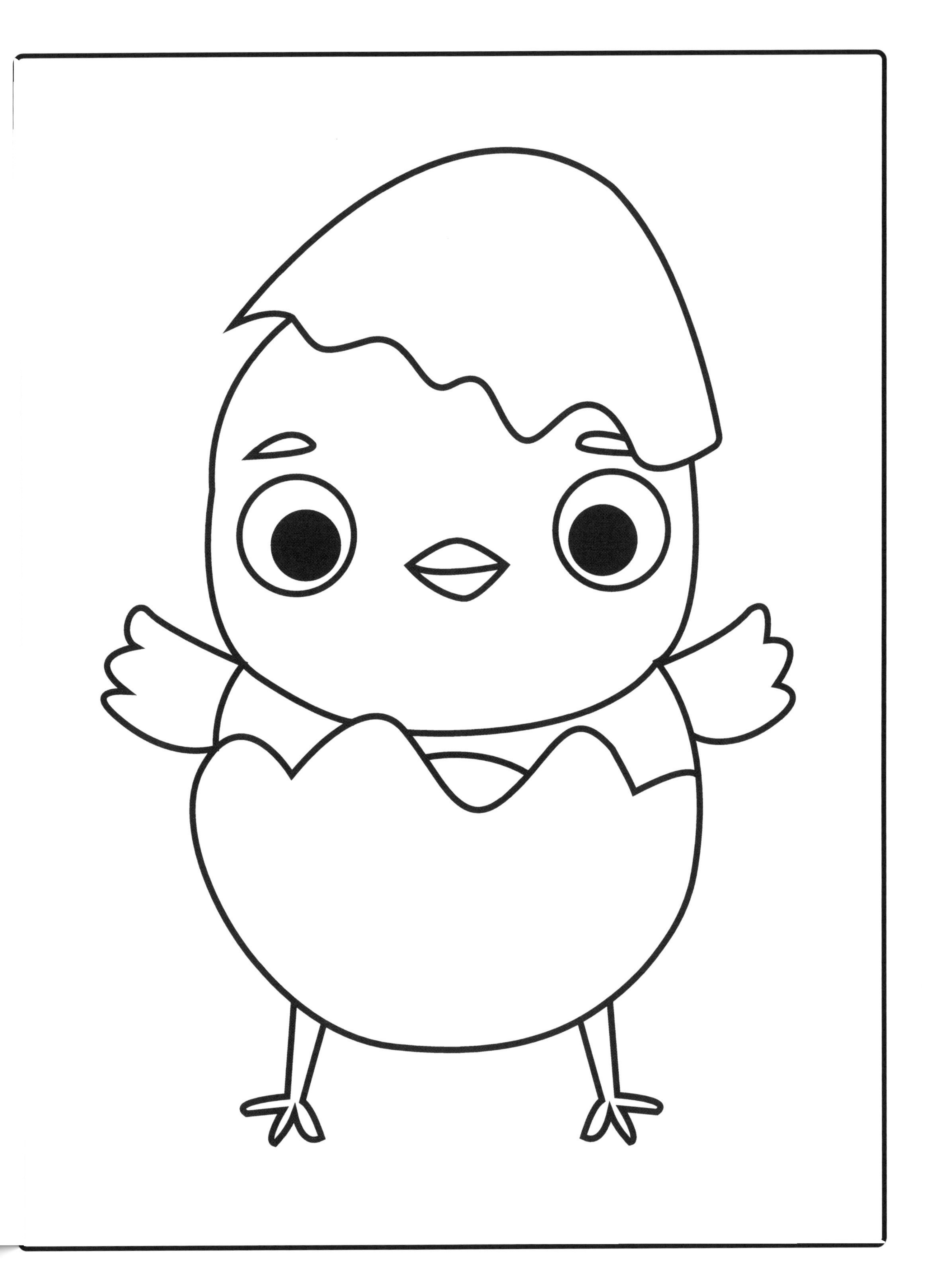

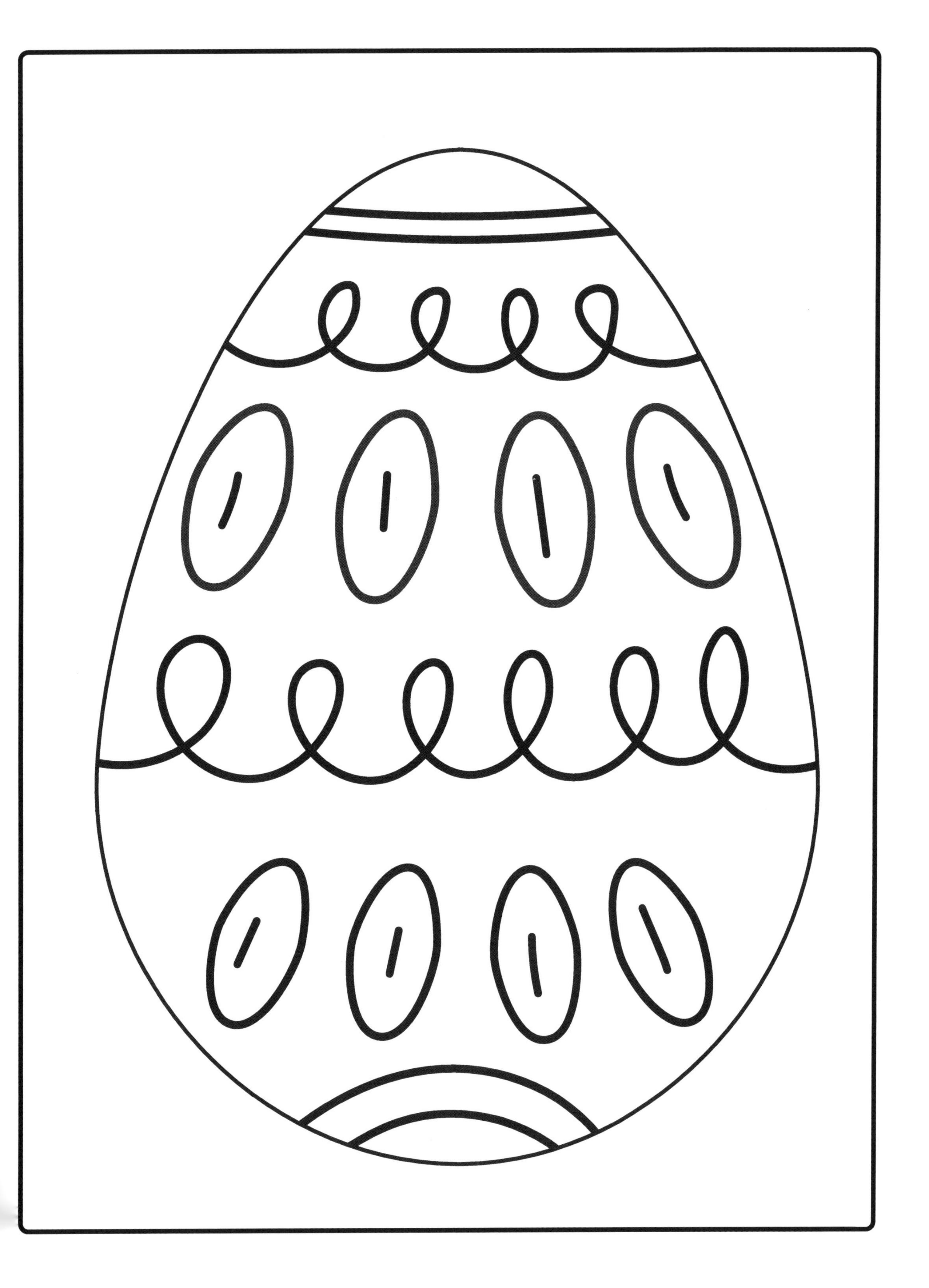

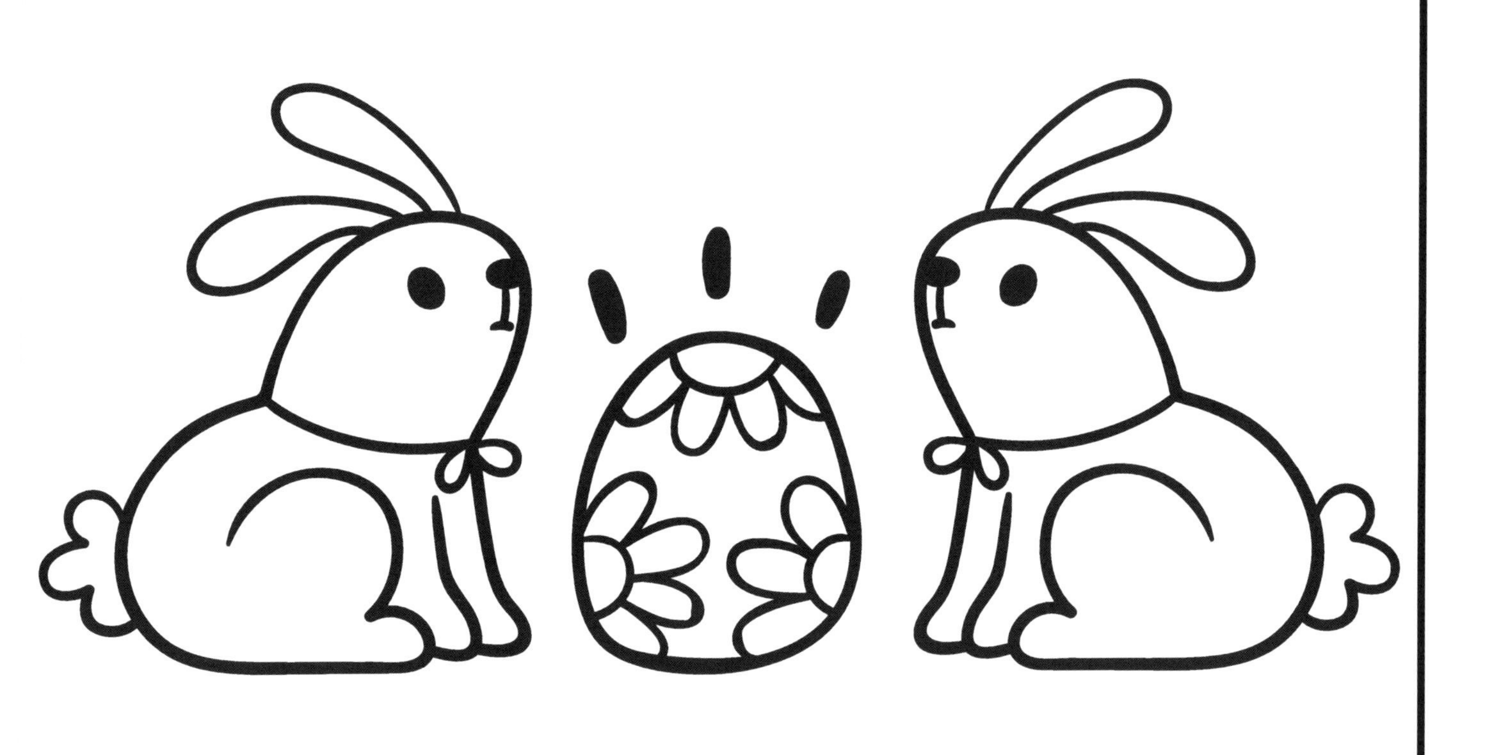

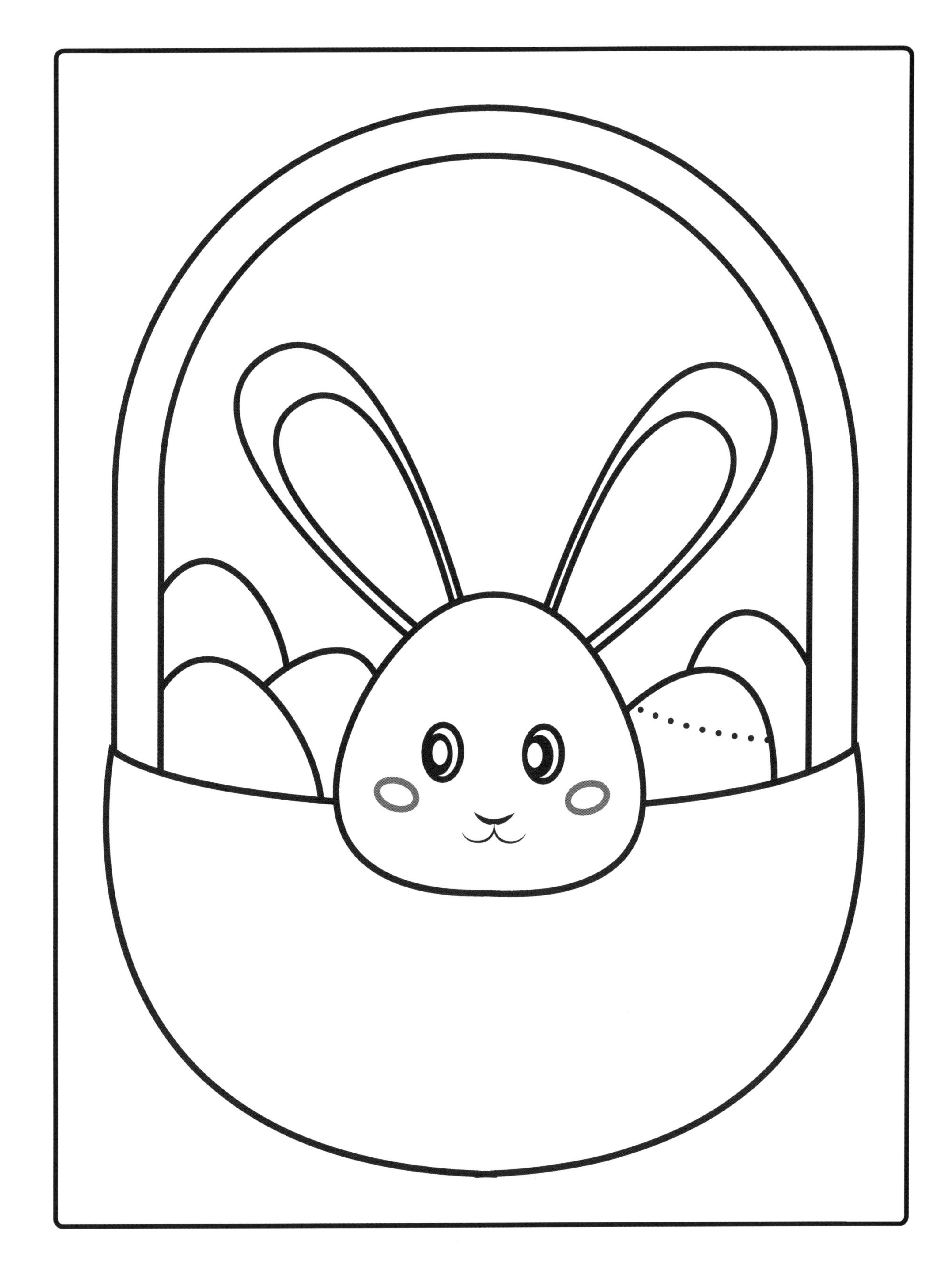

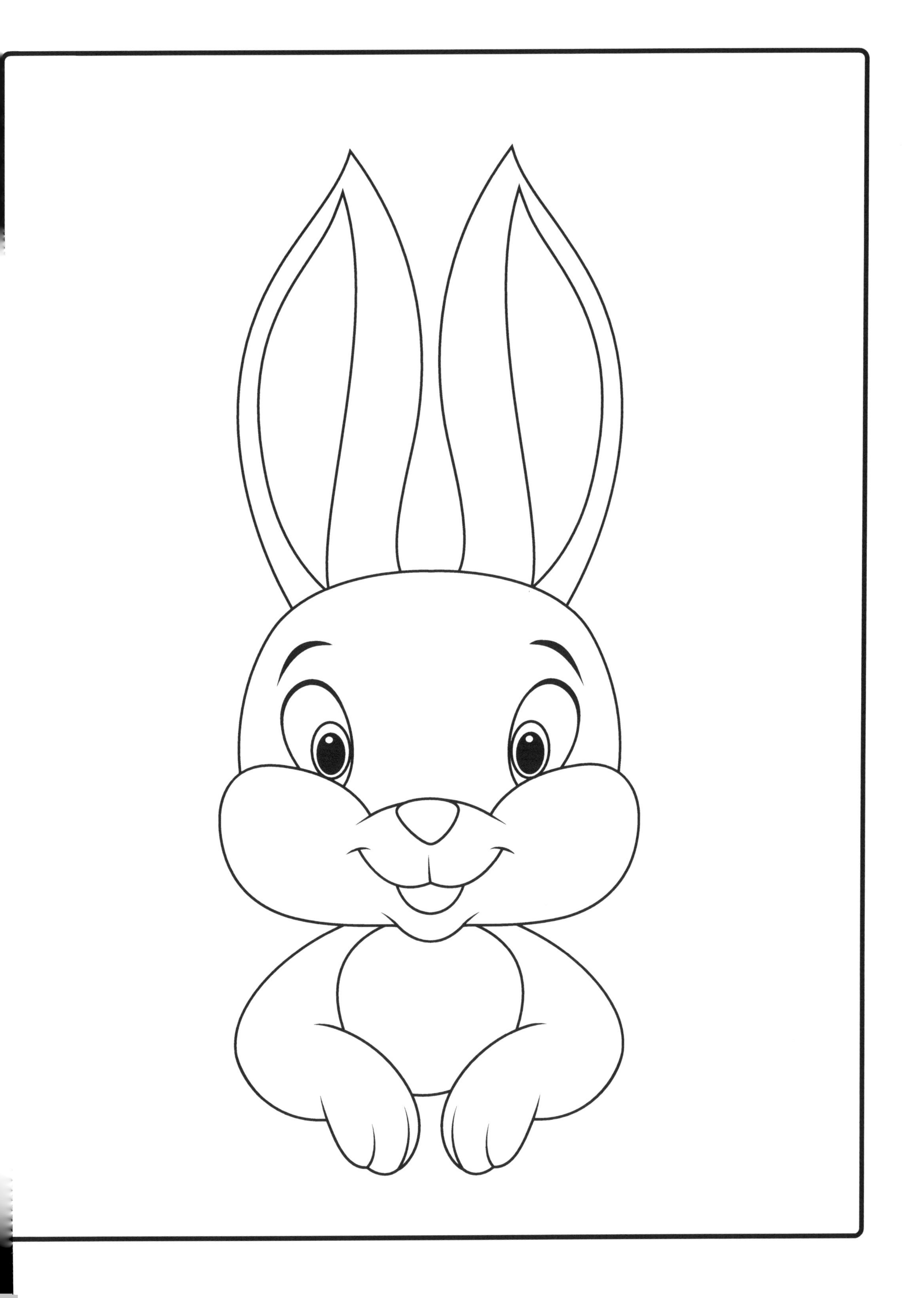

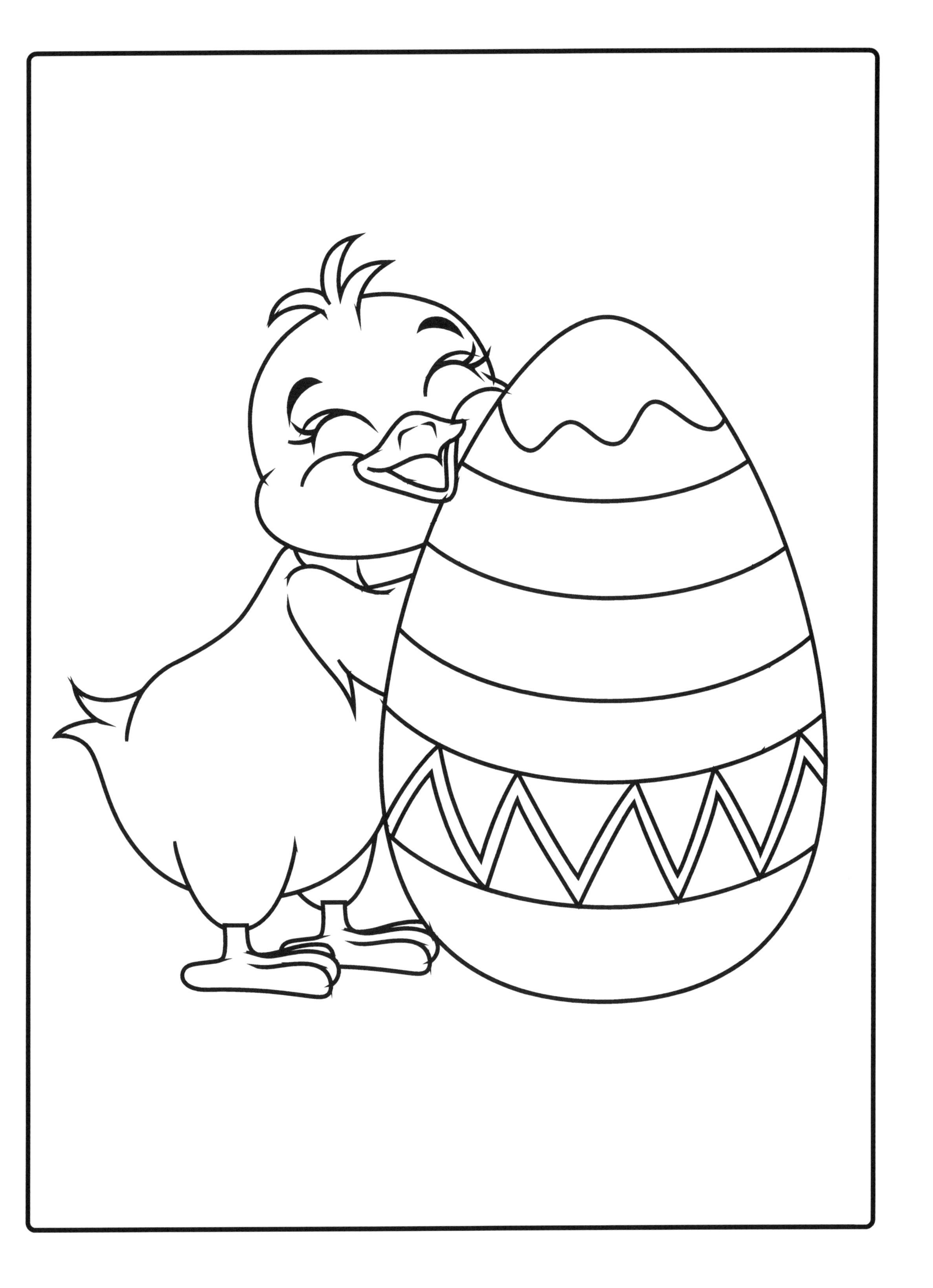

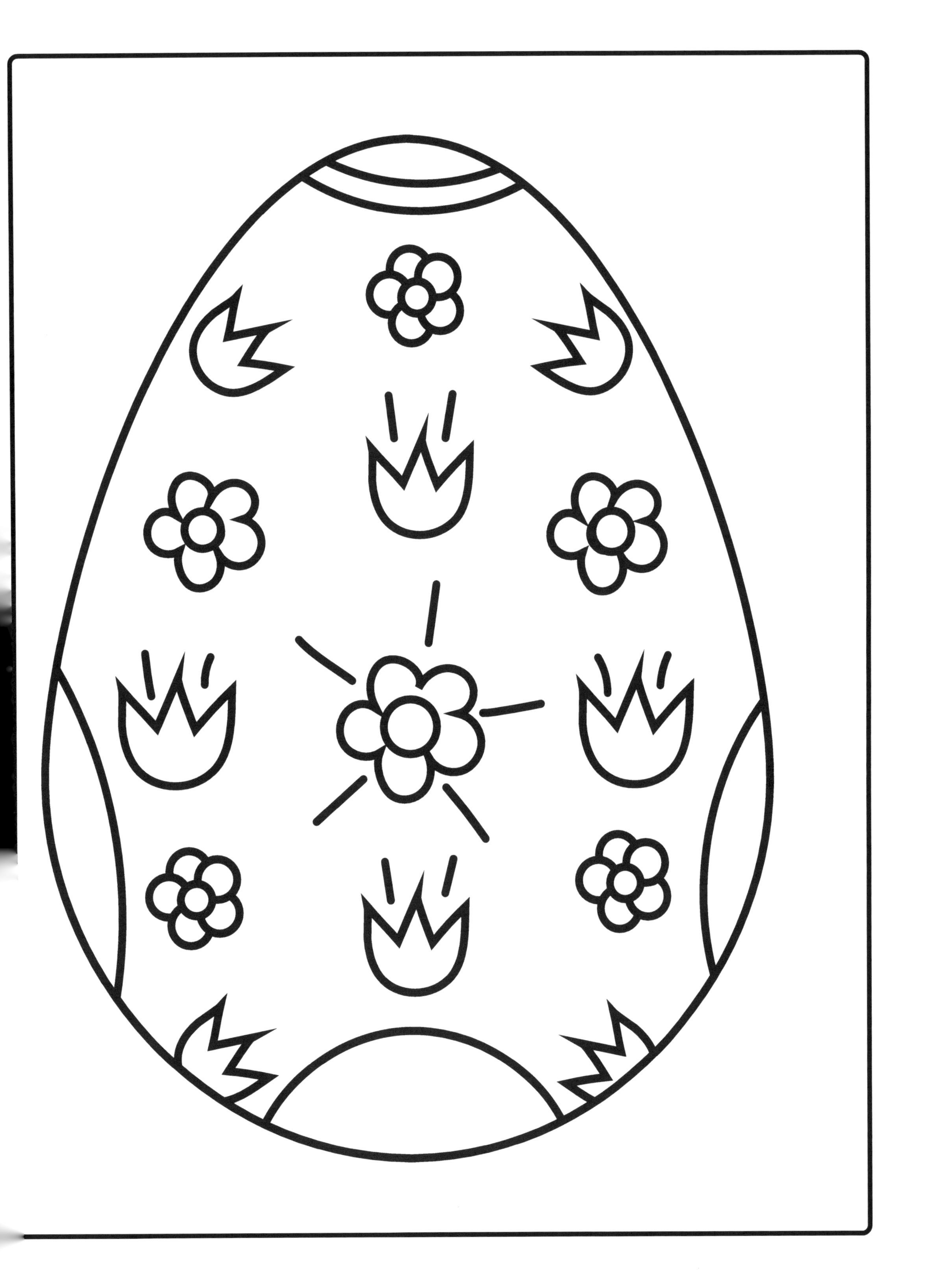

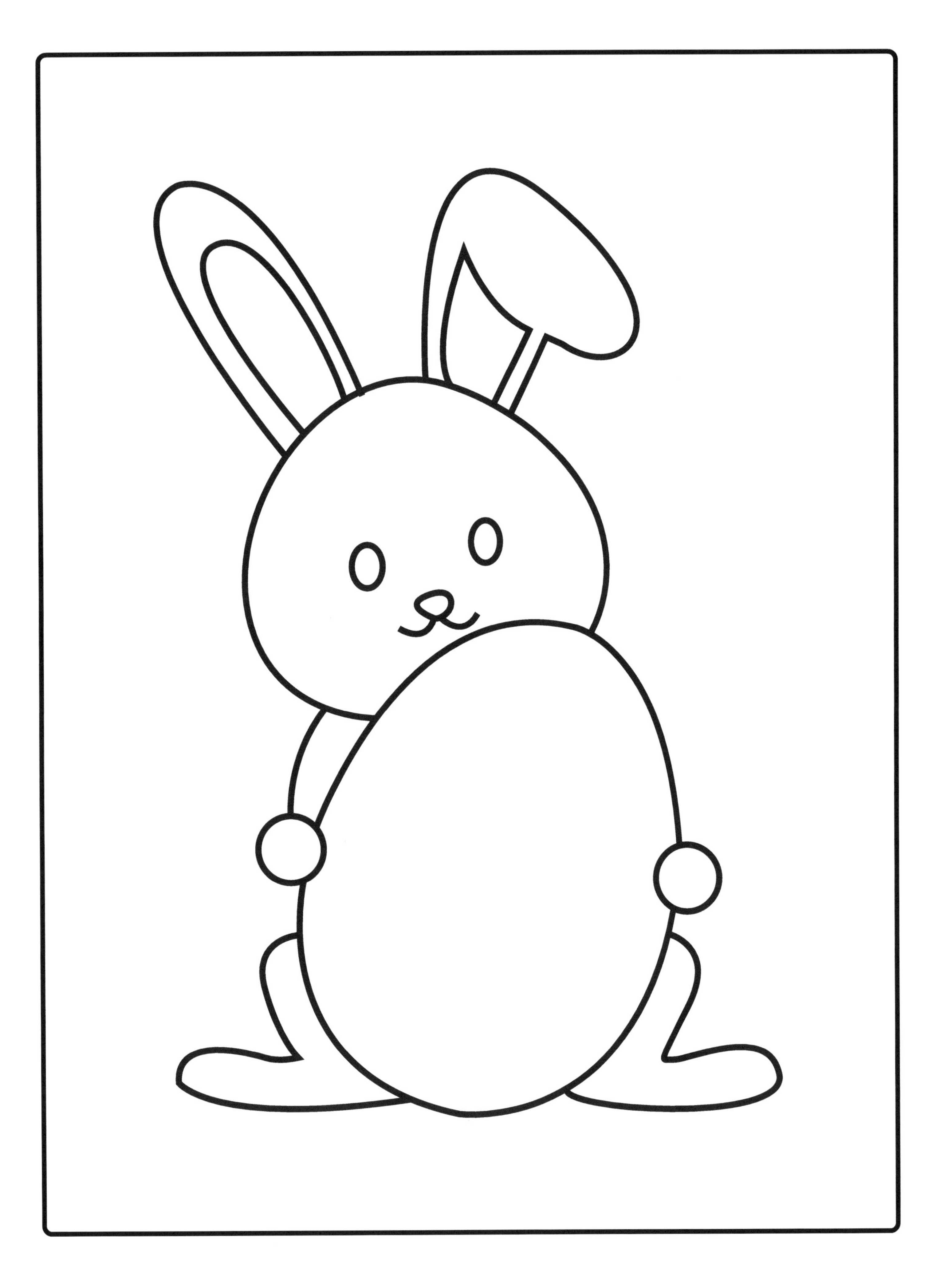

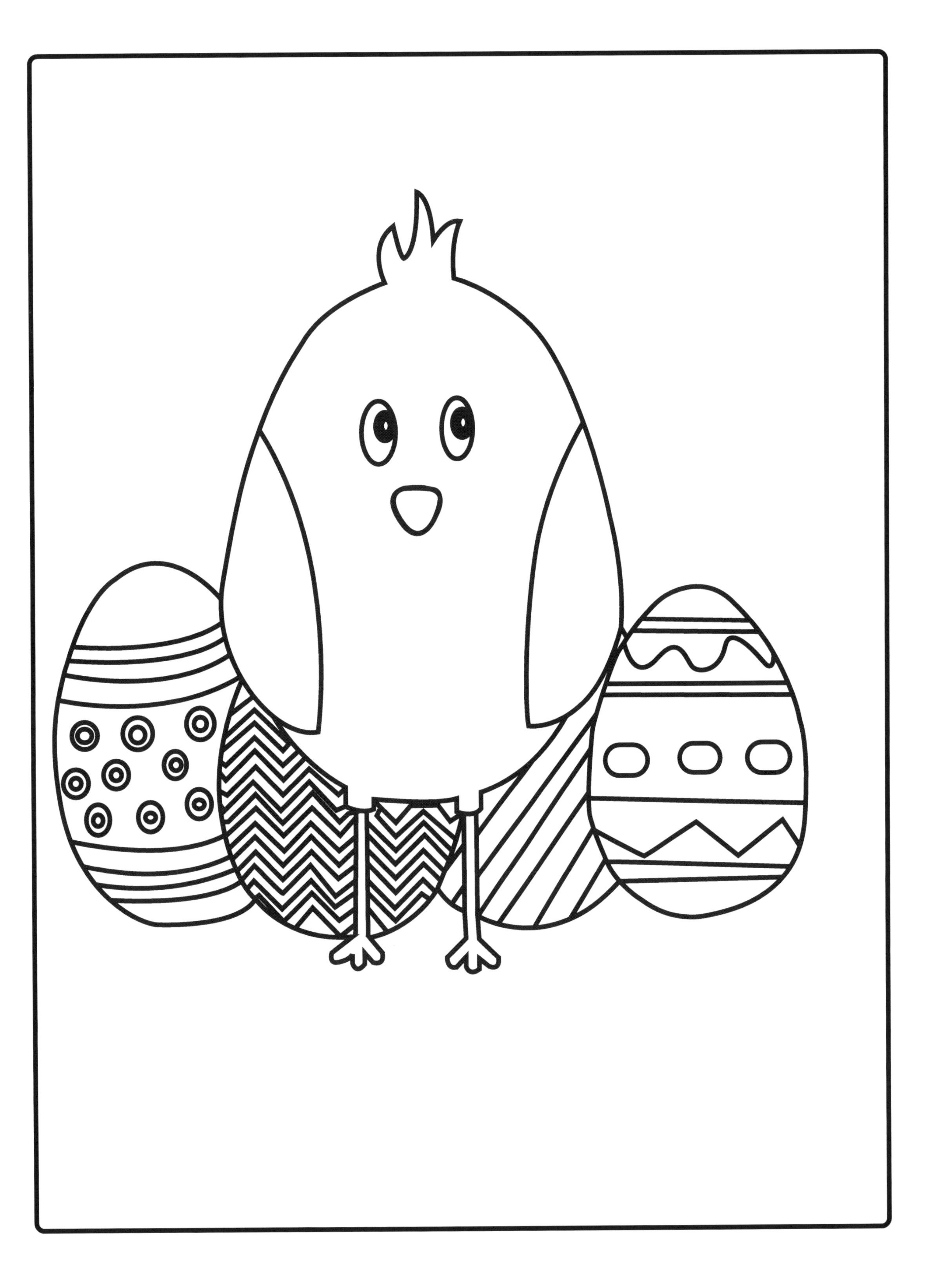

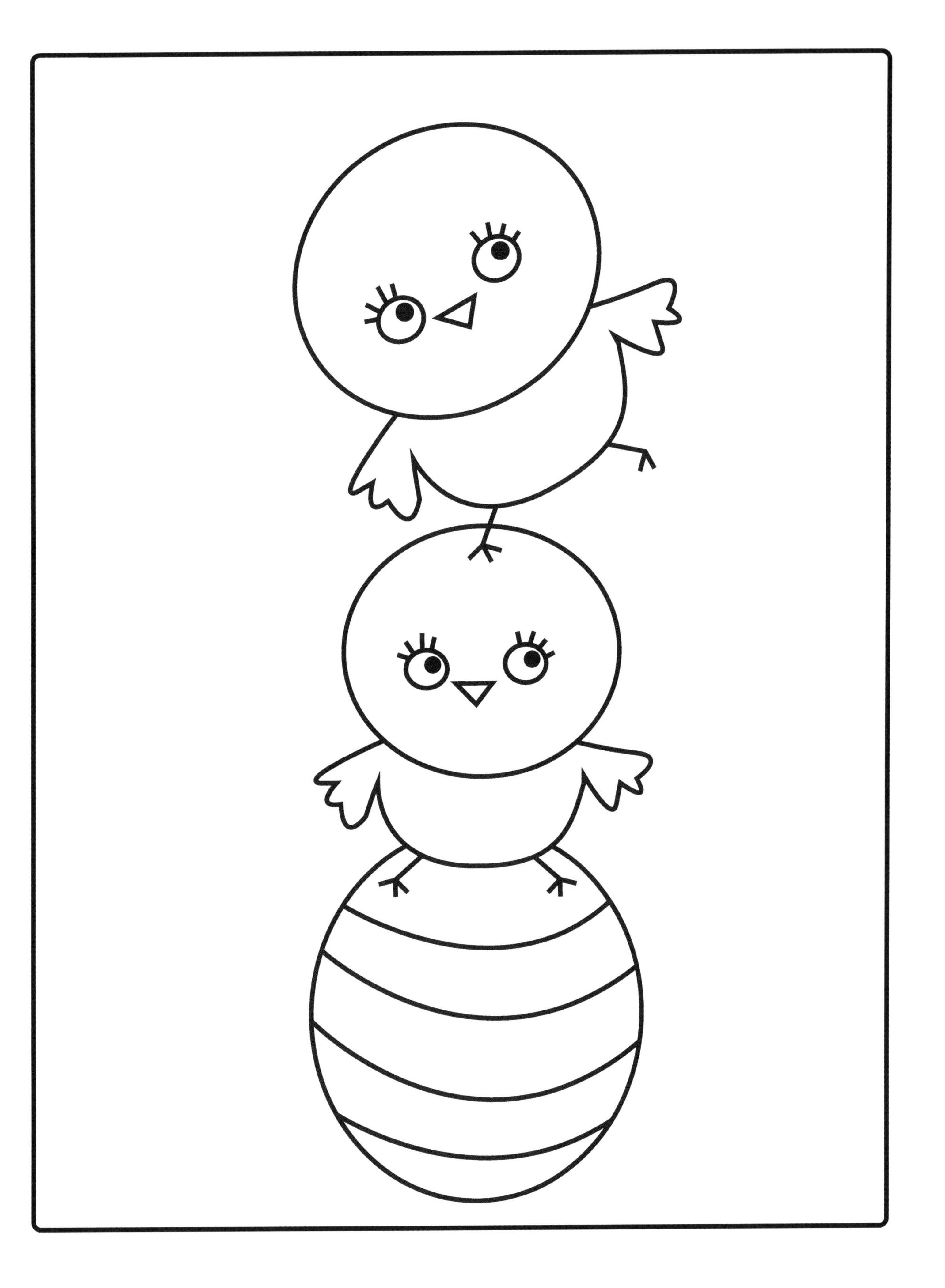

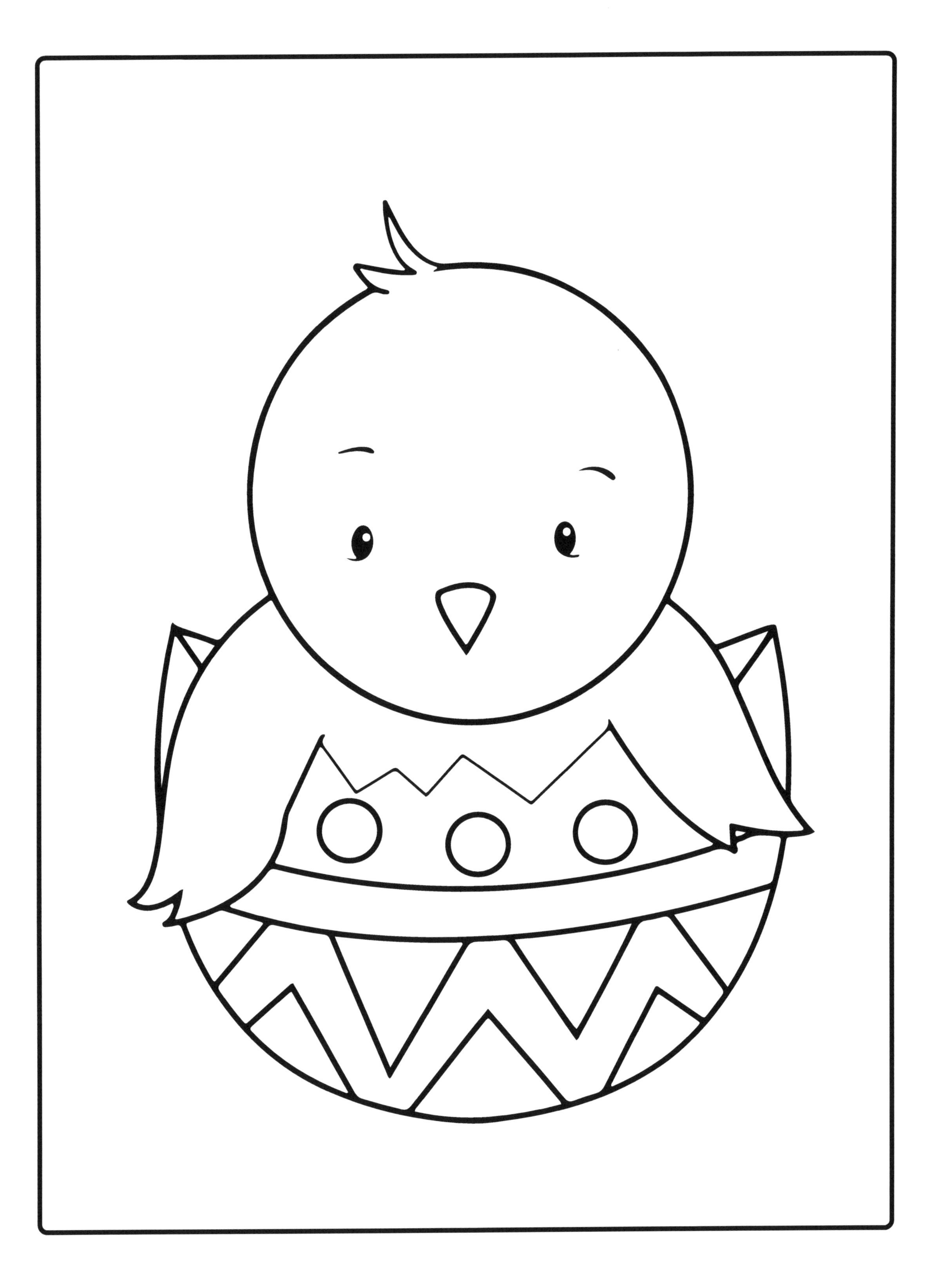

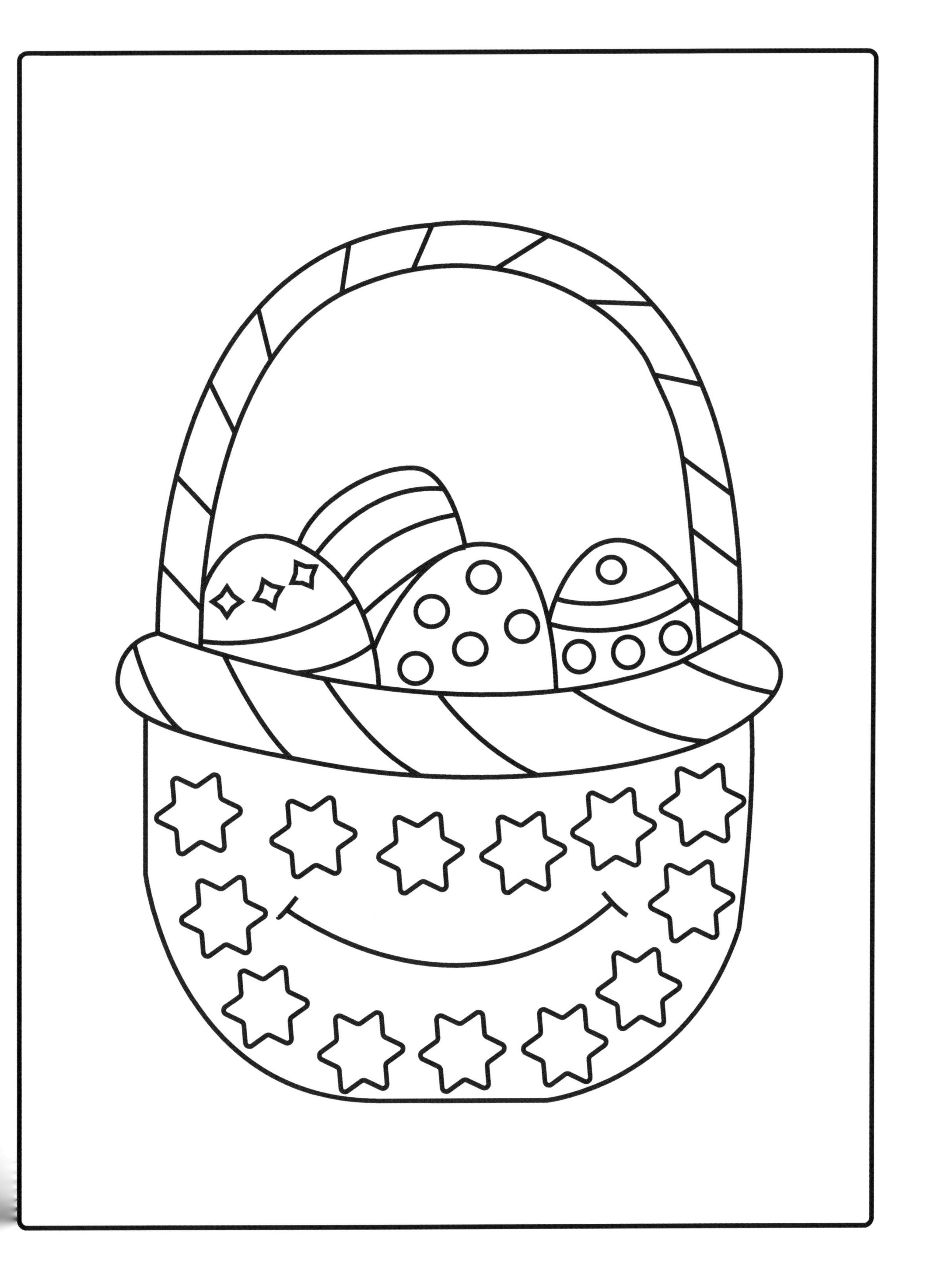

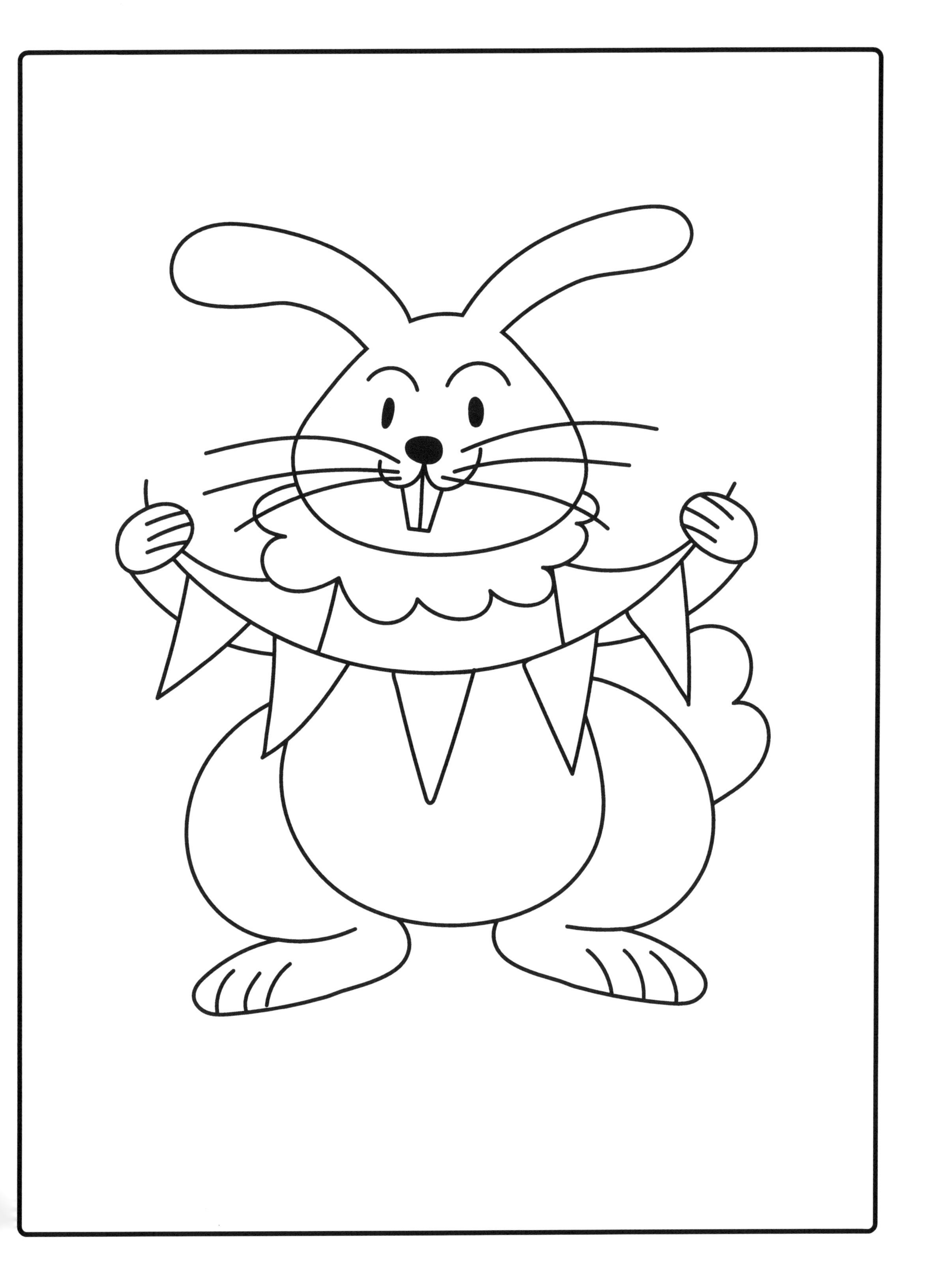

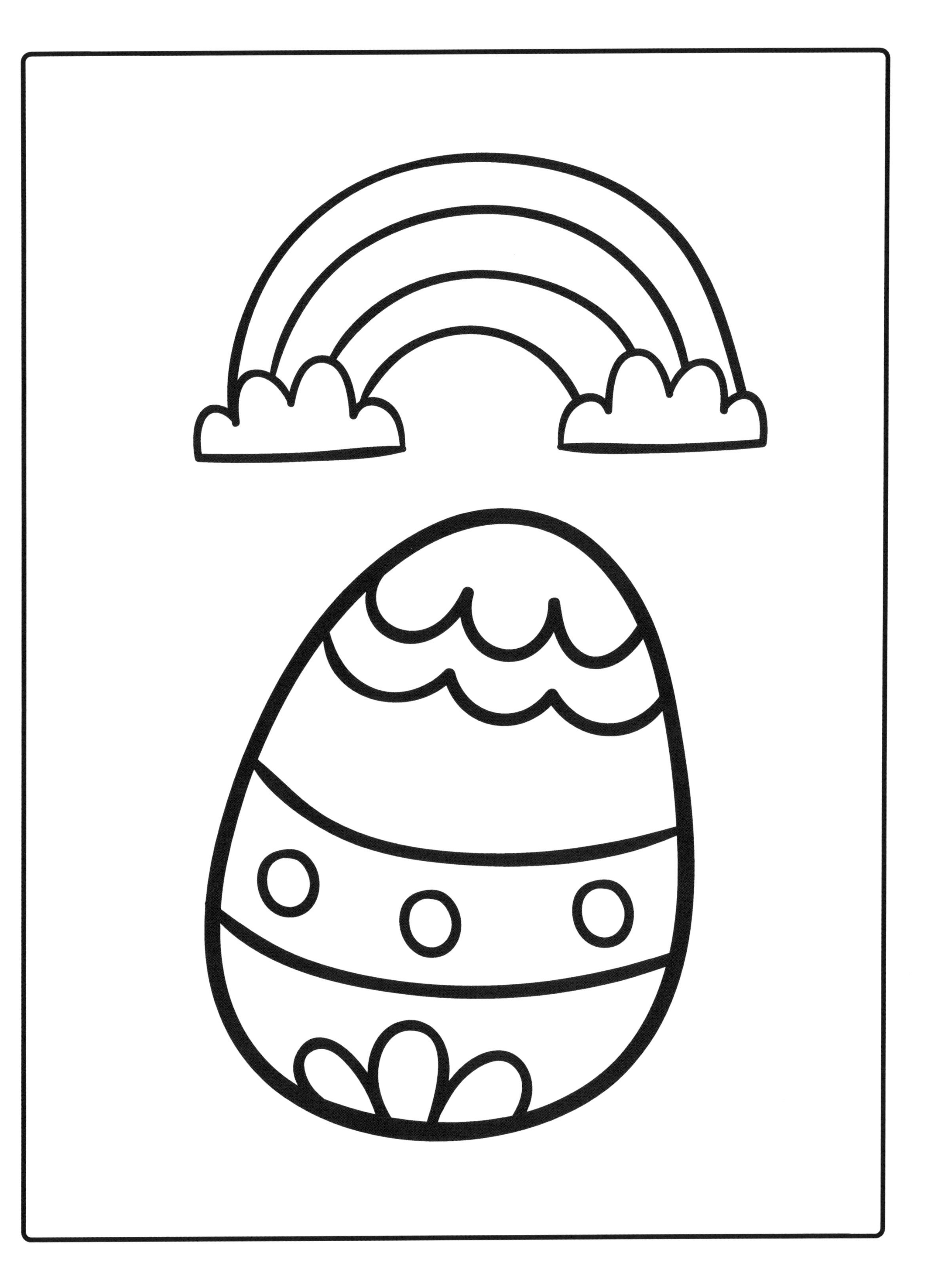

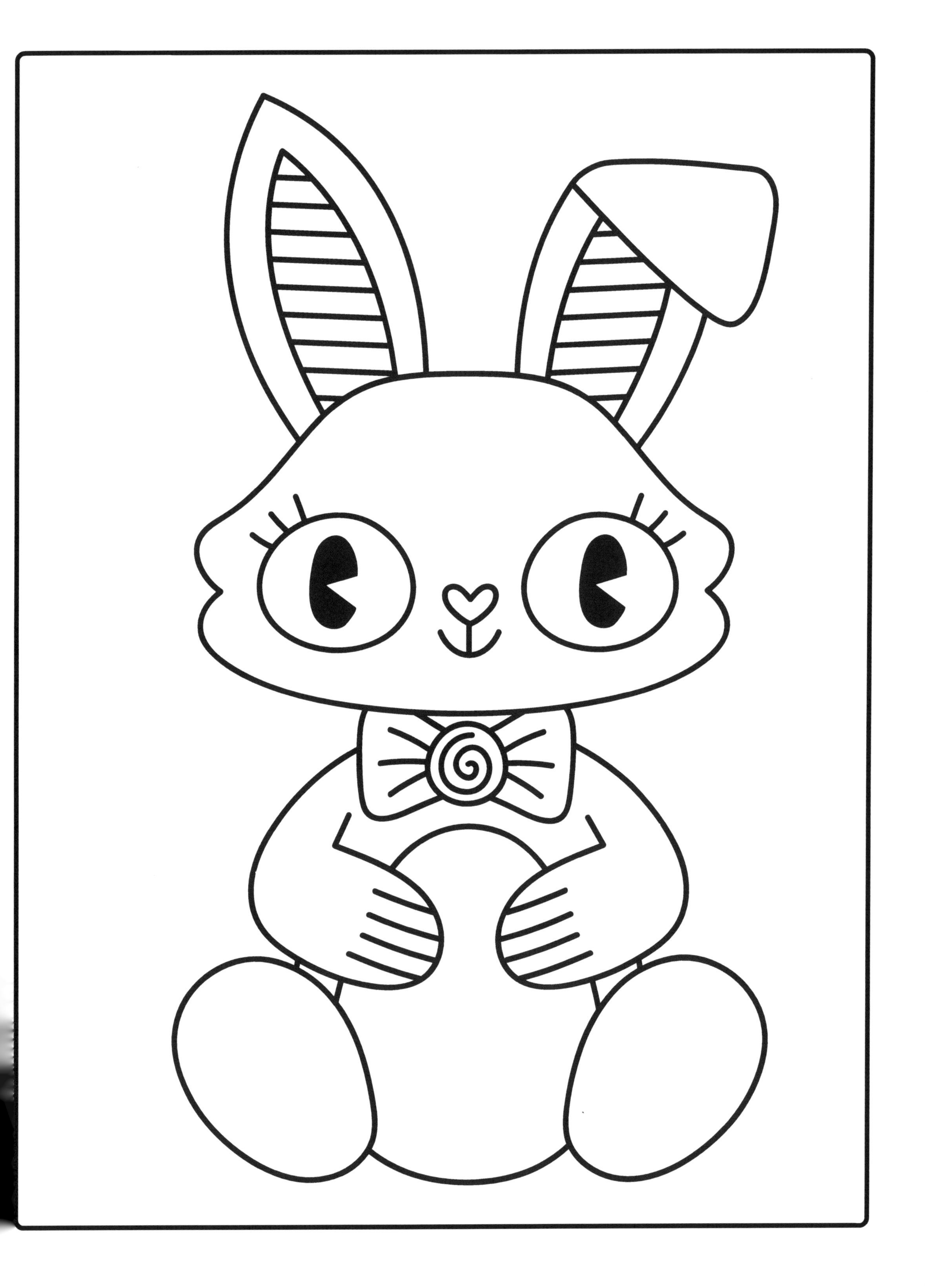

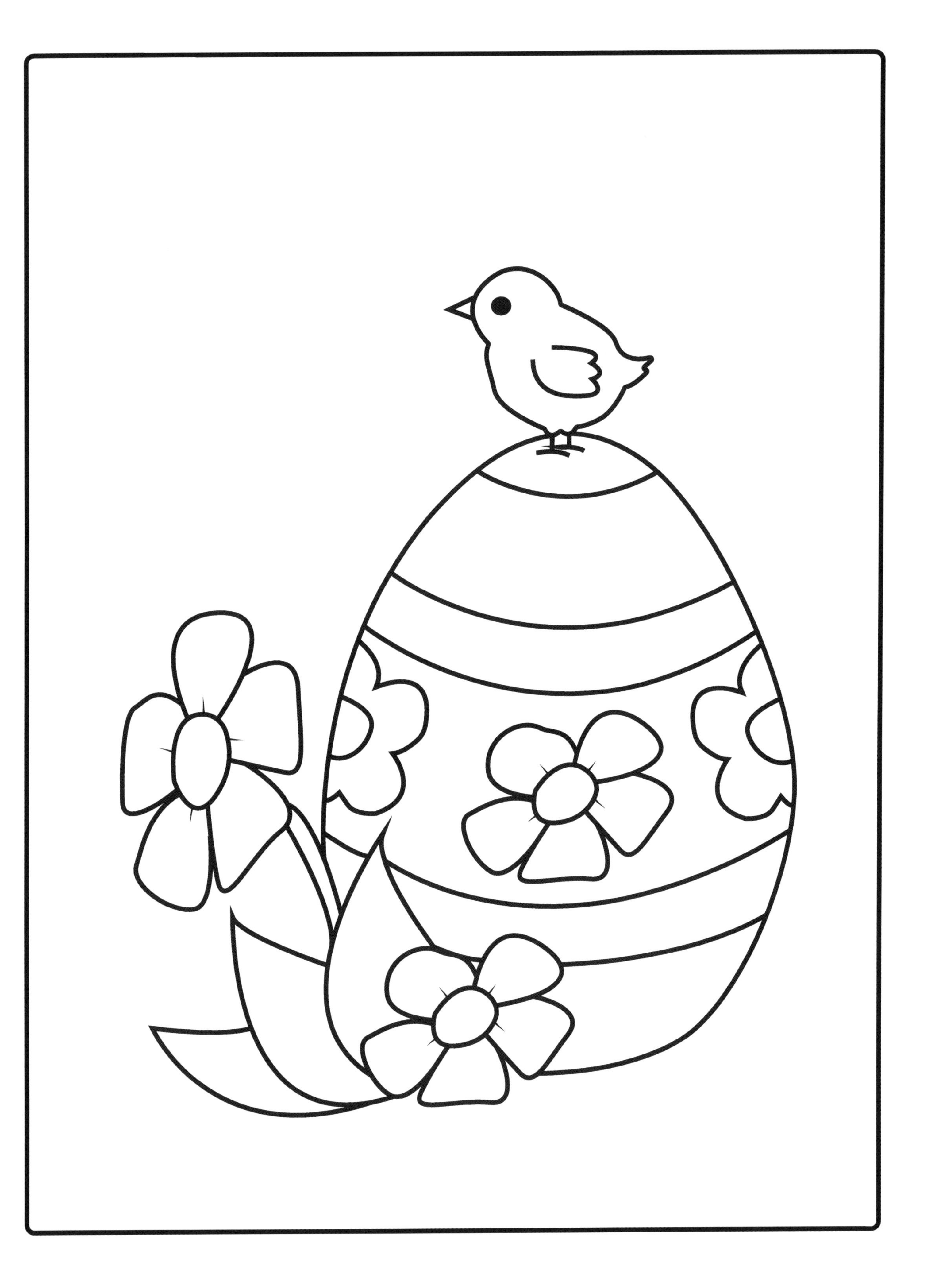

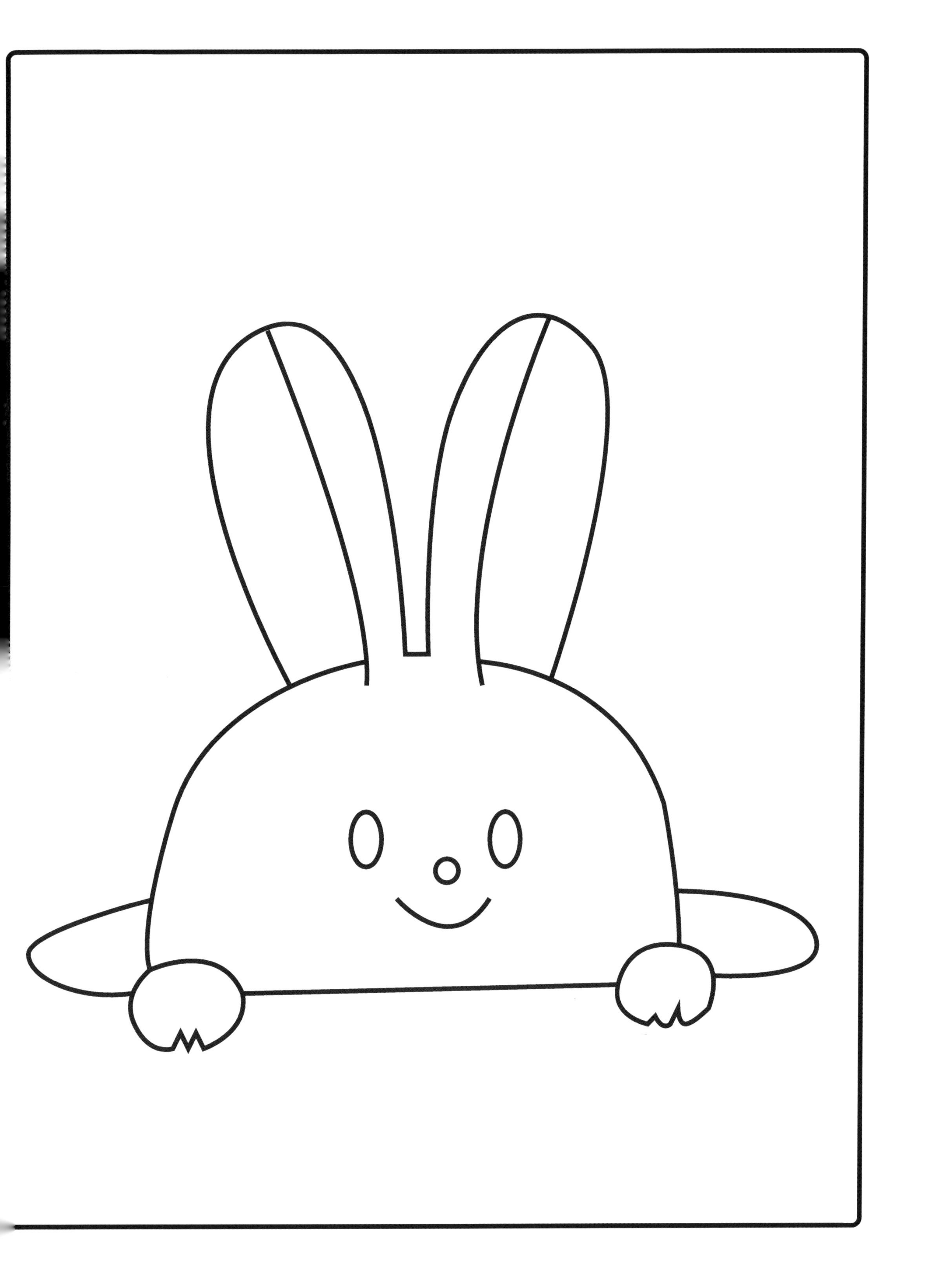

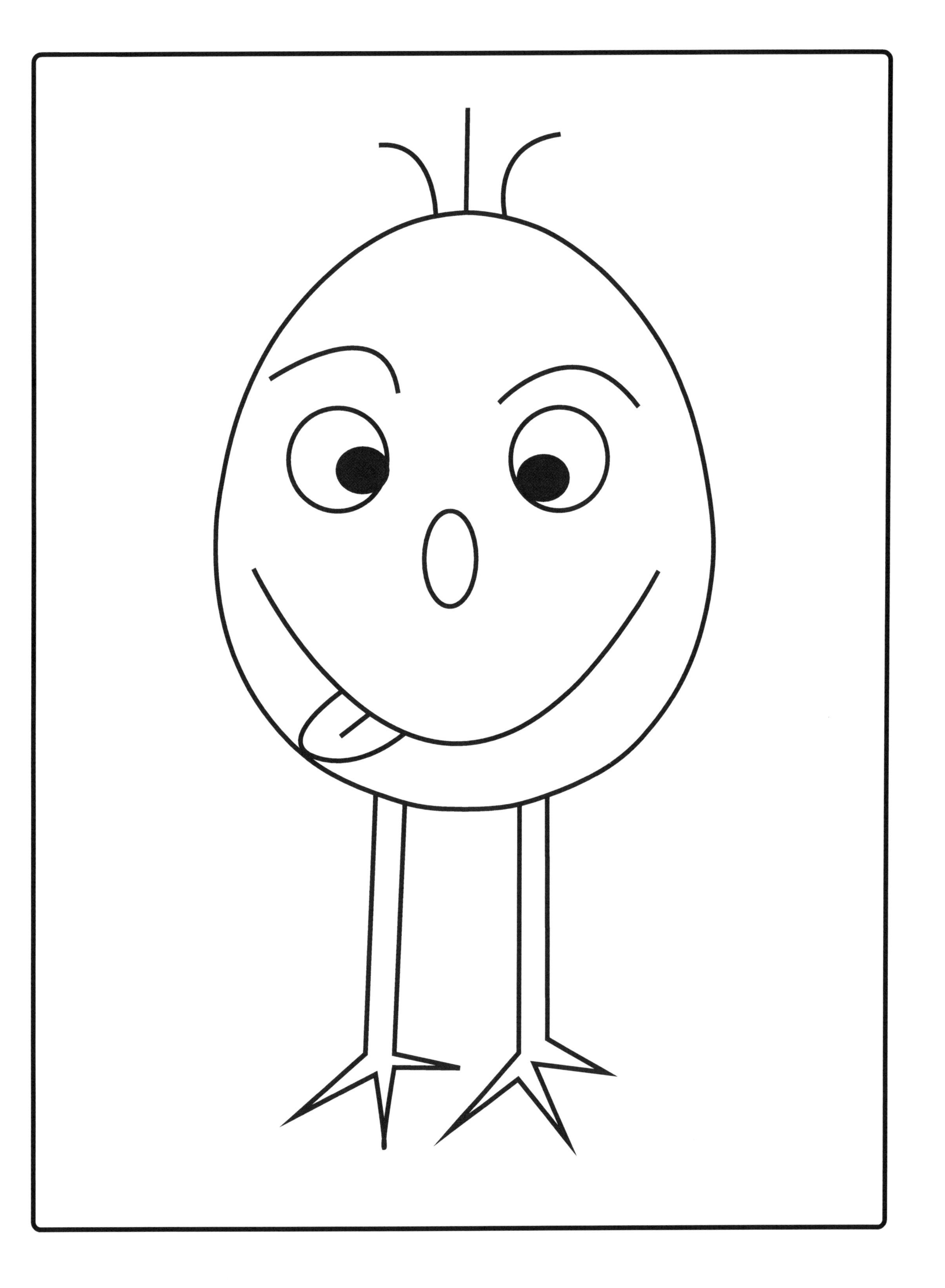

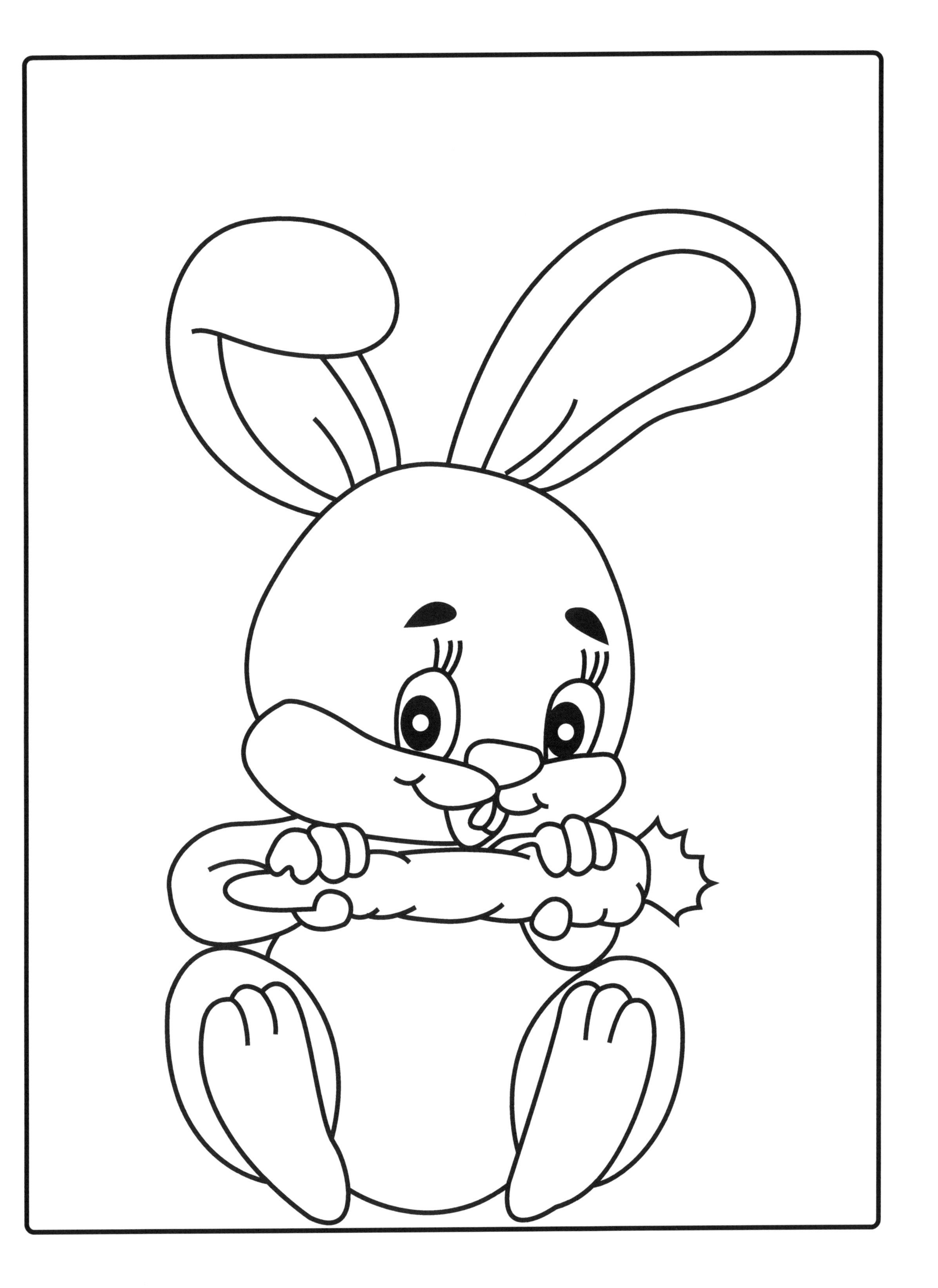

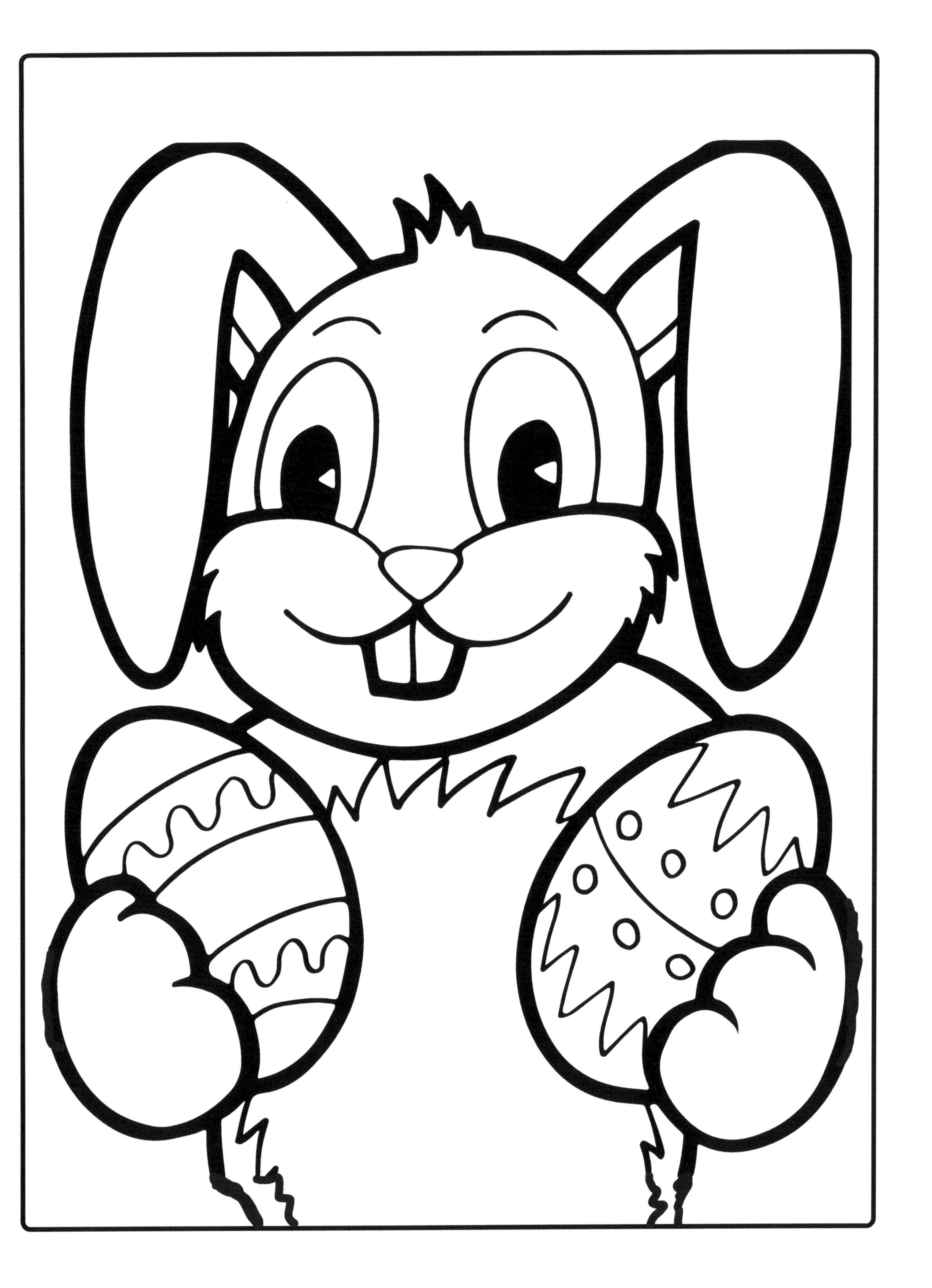

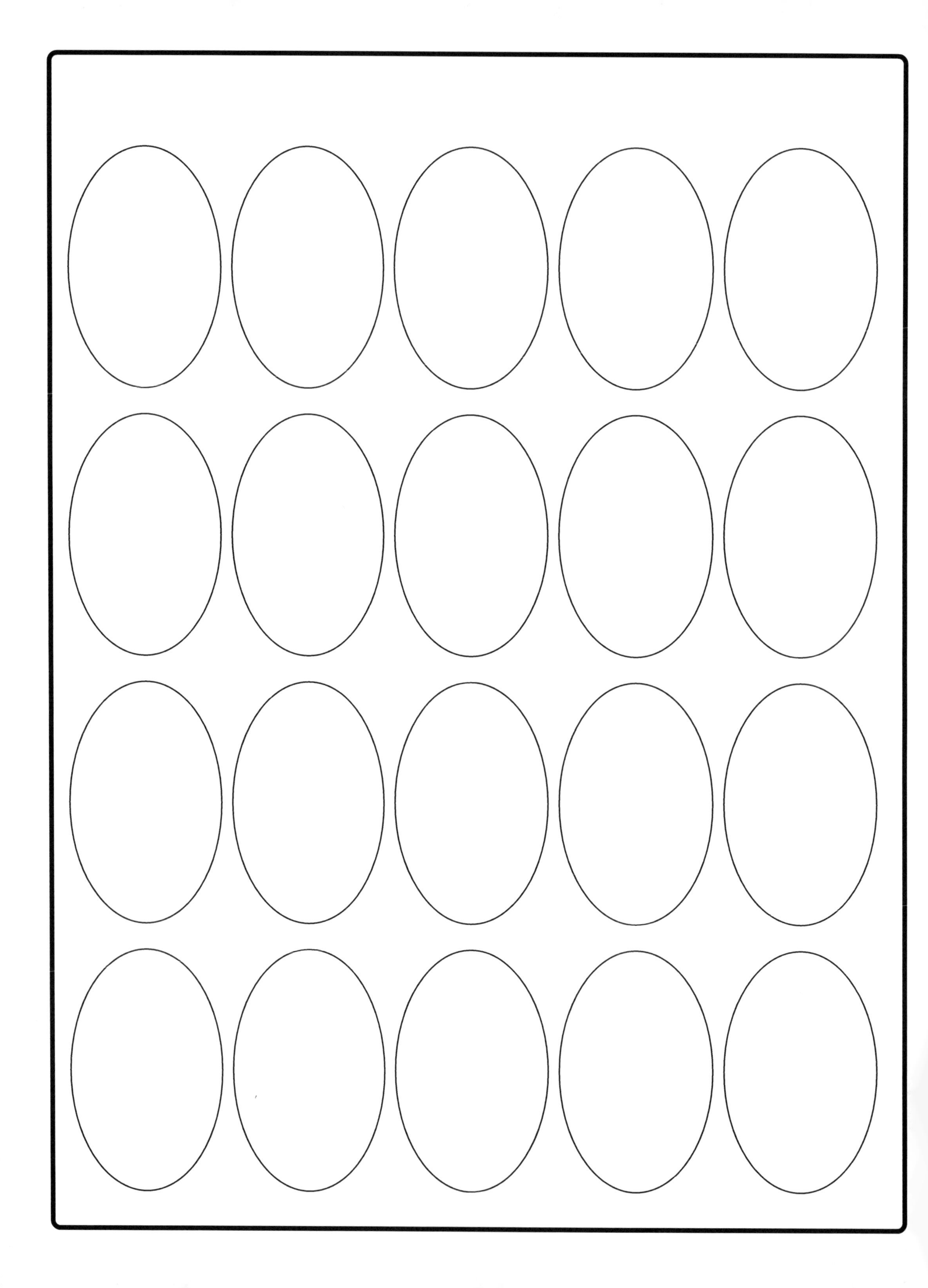

Made in the USA
Columbia, SC
12 May 2025

57833104R00057